Charles Rennie
MACKINTOSH

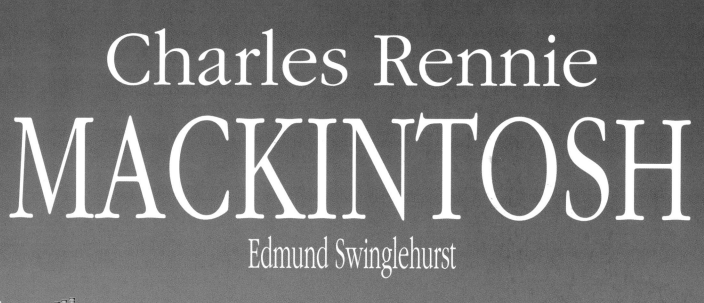

Charles Rennie
MACKINTOSH

Edmund Swinglehurst

Grange
BOOKS

Published in 2001 by
Grange Books
An imprint of Grange Books Plc
The Grange
Kingsnorth Industrial Estate
Hoo, Nr Rochester
Kent ME3 9ND

www.grangebooks.co.uk

Printed in Hong Kong

For Julian

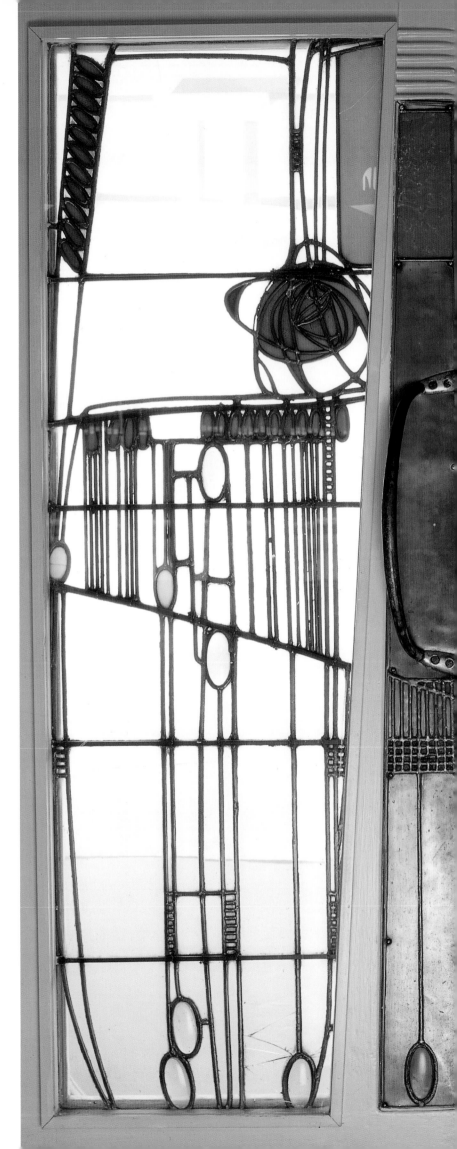

TITLE PAGE

The Martyrs' Public School: This was
Mackintosh's first building, conceived in
1895.

RIGHT

The Willow Tea Rooms: Doors to the Salon
de Luxe.

Contents

THE CHANGING SCENE

The Glasgow into which Charles Rennie Mackintosh was born on 7 June 1868 was Scotland's largest industrial city, its business concentrated mainly on coal, steel and other heavy industry, and on Glasgow's great river, the Clyde, this meant shipbuilding. The Clyde was the world's main centre for the building of the metal-hulled, propeller-driven ships that were opening up the world to trade and commerce. As the capital of this booming industry, Glasgow had a centre dominated by buildings housing the offices of some of the world's greatest names in shipping: the Anchor Line, the Clan Line, Cunard, Donaldson's, the White Star and others, which dominated the world's shipping lanes and brought foreign influences to the once-quiet Scottish port.

With the industrial and commercial growth of Glasgow, there came the same cultural changes that had been fermenting in England and which had been expressed by William Blake in *Jerusalem*, his poem of a Utopian state growing out of the dark satanic mills of industry. The rapid growth of this industrial age was preoccupying many people, who, bewildered by the unknown and terrifying world of machines, were turning to Nature as an antidote to the soulless mechanical future that seemed to be threatening human life and values.

The Romantic movement, which had its origins in the late 18th century and extended into the 19th, had seen a similar reaction in the form of a rejection of classicism and neoclassicism and the rationalism which had characterized the Enlightenment. It was exemplified in the work of Wordsworth, Byron, Shelley, Keats and Blake, in the painting of Turner, Delacroix and Goya, and in the music of Schumann, Liszt and Wagner. It also manifested itself in a mania for collecting natural objects, especially in the case of the Victorians, who littered their drawing rooms with sea shells and stuffed birds.

Nature became a defence against the encroaching machine. Thus was born, spontaneously in different parts of the world, a form of art which drew its inspiration from nature, and especially from plants. The new art forms were sinuous and curving, like growing plants themselves, and were adopted by the Pre-Raphaelite painters and by William Morris, whose designs spread far and wide. In France, the new art forms, given the name Art Nouveau, appeared in the work of Hector

Charles Rennie Mackintosh (Francis Herbert Newbery, 1914) Oil on canvas. 43$\frac{1}{2}$ x 24$\frac{3}{16}$in (110.5 x 61.4cm).

Newbery (1855–1946) was a painter as well as a teacher and was the director of the Glasgow School of Art from 1885–1917; he did much to encourage the young Mackintosh. In 1889 he married, his wife Jessie being a decorative artist in her own right. Her speciality was embroidery, which she also taught at the school.

Charles Rennie Mackintosh

Mackintosh, Romantic and Modernist was, at the age of 25, a handsome young man, with a certain style to his manner and dress. The serious, slightly anxious expression on his face may have come from a self-awareness of his physical disabilities, which have been described as a club foot and a tendency to autism. However, neither of these appear to have detracted from his vitality or innovative spirit, nor it seems from his attractiveness to women.

RIGHT
**Poster for the Glasgow
Institute of the Fine Arts**
(c.1896)
Lithograph.

This poster is similar to
the one that Mackintosh
produced for the *Scottish
Musical Review* (page
11); however, this one
was a collaboration of
Mackintosh with Herbert
McNair and the
Macdonald sisters,
Margaret and Frances.
The four friends often
worked on projects
together and became
known as The Four. Like
Toulouse-Lautrec in
France and Aubrey
Beardsley in London, they
were intent on creating a
unique style of their own.

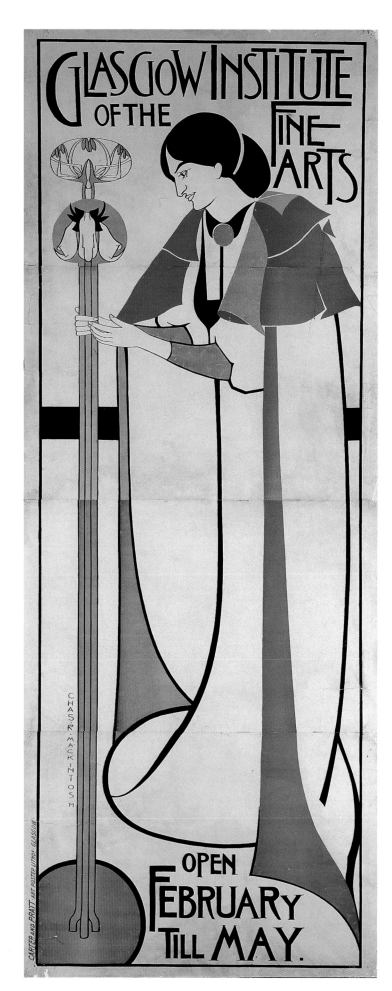

OPPOSITE
**The Glasgow School of
Art**

A sculpture class,
photographed around
1900.

Guimard, whose Paris Métro stations remain as his monument; in Vienna in the buildings of Josef Hoffmann and Kolomon Moser; and in Holland in those of Victor Horta. In New York, Louis Comfort Tiffany, whose stained-glass lamps are found attractive today, was an exponent of American Art Nouveau.

These innovators harboured no nostalgic feelings for the past, but set out to find a way in which the worlds of nature and the machine could be harmonized to the benefit of mankind: Blake's *Jerusalem*, in fact.

In Scotland, the man who most believed in and promoted these new ideals was Charles Rennie Mackintosh. He was raised a Presbyterian, with strict codes of morality, and had all the stubborn determination of his race. It was he, with several friends, who in Scotland created the form of Art Nouveau which became known as the original Glasgow style.

Mackintosh, the son of a police clerk, was sent to Reid's Public School and then to Allan Glen's High School, a private school for the sons of artisans and tradesmen, where a conventional curriculum encouraged dedication, hard work and a practical and vocational approach to learning, and where mathematical tables were printed in the back of prayer books.

Mackintosh was an adaptable and obedient pupil but, having a defect in one foot which made him limp, no doubt felt himself at a disadvantage. This may have made him more withdrawn, and his already reclusive nature made it difficult for him to communicate easily with others; but at the same time, he was determined to succeed. It has recently been suggested that Mackintosh may have been autistic, but his stubborn singlemindedness may simply have been the product of his Scottish origins and, as with many other individualistic and creative people, the natural outcome of his genius.

In 1884, at the age of 16, Mackintosh was apprenticed to an architect, John Hutchison, and also began to attend classes at the Glasgow School of Art. He continued to study there until 1894. Two years later, in 1896, his employer at that time, the architectural firm of John Honeyman and Keppie, gave him the task of drawing up plans for a new Glasgow School of Art.

While at the Glasgow School of Art, Mackintosh had become aware of the new trends in art and design in continental Europe, and especially in France, with which Scotland had had a long and sympathetic bond. He also absorbed ideas from Patrick Geddes, a friend and social philosopher, who introduced Mackintosh to the concept of towns and cities as entities possessing a life and identity of their own, which architects and especially planners should take into account. This was a new idea at a time when urban conurbations were spreading at a rapid and chaotic pace because of the demands of industrial life.

Mackintosh was particularly inspired by the designs of William Morris and the writings of John Ruskin, who saw the black tide of industry engulfing the traditional view that Nature reflected a God-inspired plan.

They, and others like them, were leading a crusade to establish a working relationship between Nature and the industrial world, a culture in which the advances of technology would be linked to the world of art. From this was to grow the Art Nouveau movement, in which natural forms would be translated to iron and glass.

Geddes' ideas made a deep impression on Mackintosh and his friends, Herbert McNair and Margaret and Frances Macdonald, who were fellow artists looking to the future. They firmly believed that recycled versions of Greek and Roman art and architecture were no longer relevant.

They had an ally in the new director of the Glasgow School of Art, Francis Newbery, an enlightened and visionary man who encouraged his talented students, soon to be known as The Four. Newbery was also excited by the new ideas concerning the importance of harmonizing buildings with their interiors and helped to create the influential interior design department, whose influence through the Glasgow Art Club soon spread across the English Channel.

Constant attendance at the Glasgow School of Art was not compulsory and The Four were able to work together on projects outside the school curriculum, designing posters, items of furniture and much else. Their collaboration was particularly stimulating and allowed them to develop new ideas and to exhibit their work.

Very soon, they began to be noticed at Art and Craft exhibitions, both in London and abroad, and including Vienna

and Munich, both important centres of the Art Nouveau movement, where they had been encouraged to exhibit after their first showing at Liège in 1895.

McNair and the Macdonald sisters created a number of small articles of furniture, such as a mirror in beaten lead on a wooden frame which they entitled *Vanity*, and a wooden screen called *Birth and Death of Winds*. Mackintosh designed an elegant hall settle which was made by Guthrie and Wells, and a washstand made of green stained oak, the idea for which he had borrowed from a Pre-Raphaelite painting by Ford Madox Brown.

All of them produced a number of decorative posters at this time, characterized by the long flowing lines of Art Nouveau and echoing the work of Aubrey Beardsley, who was the master of the style in England. The Four were beginning to make their mark on the Continental world of art and architecture.

ABOVE

The Glasgow School of Art

Students attending a drawing class in the museum, around 1900.

RIGHT

Poster for *The Scottish Musical Review*
(c.1896)
Lithograph.

This poster, created by Mackintosh, was made with little knowledge of the technique, but was an original concept at the time, and was influenced by the Art Nouveau style. It has all the freedom of the work of a graphic designer, rather than of a trained typographer.

THE FORMATIVE YEARS

Mackintosh took his first cultural tour abroad in 1891, as a result of winning a scholarship; but he was already forming clear ideas concerning the course his own work would take. He had decided to discard the outworn traditions of Greece and Rome, the fluted columns and decorated pediments which were still the text book exemplars in England, and had made a study of traditional Scottish baronial architecture, with its relationship to medieval buildings and their solid masses. Moreover, on his travels abroad, and while paying conventional homage to the Renaissance in Italy, he had been particularly drawn to the monuments of the medieval and Byzantine periods.

Appropriately, he began his four-month sojourn in Sicily, where the Norman conquerors under Roger de Hauteville had left their powerful imprint on the exotic orientalism of its former Arab occupiers. Later had come the Hohenstaufens, some of whom had ruled as Holy Roman emperors, whose powerful medieval structures and designs, based on natural forms, struck a chord in Mackintosh's mind concerning his own concepts of artistic harmony.

The Daily Record Building (1901)

RIGHT and BELOW
One of the earliest architectural designs Mackintosh made for his employers was for the *Daily Record* newspaper office. It was an opportunity to show his talent, for Honeyman was about to retire and Keppie was more interested in draftsmanship than design. Though there was little scope for original work, Mackintosh produced a clean-cut, modern design.

From Sicily Mackintosh travelled to Siena, in Tuscany, the centre of medieval linear design, which reached its apogee with Simone Martini, whose elongated figures with their undulating lines were forerunners of the flowing style of the Pre-Raphaelites and of Art Nouveau.

In Venice Mackintosh again recognized the oriental influence in the ogival curves of the windows of the Doges' Palace, the curling spires of St Mark's and in the early palazzi on the Grand Canal. In Ravenna, south of Venice along the Adriatic coast, and once the capital of the Byzantine Empire, Mackintosh found more inspiration in the mosaics of the church of San Vitale and the basilica of Sant' Appollinare in Classe.

On Mackintosh's return to Glasgow, The Four launched a magazine to promote their ideas. Simply called *The Magazine*, it contained articles and illustrations by each of them and also by their friends. Like the *Ver Sacrum* of their Viennese counterparts, the magazine found little public support and there were only three editions. Mackintosh's contributions

Craigie Hall, Bellahouston (1892–93)

Craigie Hall had originally been built in 1872 by Honeyman and Keppie who were asked to refurbish it 20 years later. Young Mackintosh, a newcomer to the firm, was entrusted with some of the design features, including the neat polished case of this small organ (LEFT), whose pipes can be seen on either side of the central structure. It clearly has Art Nouveau influences, with its symbolic oval between the doors and the sinuous lines of the central pillar.

RIGHT
Library seats embellished with scrolling foliage by Mackintosh.

ABOVE
This is one of a number of doorcases in the hallway of Craigie Hall, with decorations that suggest it is the work of Keppie's assistant, Charles Rennie Mackintosh.

OPPOSITE
The Harvest Moon
(1892)
Pencil and watercolour.
$13^{7}/_{8}$ x $10^{7}/_{8}$in (35.2 x 27.6cm).

While performing his duties as a designer and draftsman at Honeyman and Keppie, Mackintosh found time to develop his watercolour technique and to pursue the Symbolist ideas that he had encountered in Europe. This mutual interest brought Margaret Macdonald and himself together and caused him to break off his relationship with Jessie Keppie, his employer's sister. Not a communicative man, Mackintosh often expressed his innermost thoughts in pictures such as these. The upright figure highlighted against the golden orb and the prostrate figure in a field of thorns seems to echo his personal dilemma.

LEFT
Charles Rennie Mackintosh and Hamish Davidson

Hamish Davidson was the son of William Davidson, who commissioned Mackintosh to design a detached house for him which was completed late in 1901. It was called Windyhill (p. 90–93).

included a watercolour, *Cabbages in an Orchard*, and two symbolic works, *The Tree of Personal Effort* and *The Tree of Influence* (p. 18 and 19).

Though so far, graphic design had taken up a great deal of Mackintosh's time and attention, his ambitions still lay in the field of architecture. His work for Honeyman and Keppie was in this field, and though he was obliged to work within the context of his employers' ideas, which tended to conform to the existing fashion in Glasgow, he planned one day to design a building of his own. As Honeyman was an elderly man and John Keppie, a recent partner in the firm, was more interested in draftsmanship than design, Mackintosh

foresaw that he would gradually have an opportunity to introduce his own ideas.

His European travels, his study of Scottish baronial architecture, and his familiarity with the architecture of his own time in Glasgow had set new parameters for him concerning the possibilities of original design. Like Ruskin and Pugin in England and George Baldwin Brown in Edinburgh, Mackintosh had come to believe in an architecture that met the practical requirements of a building and also in the need for respecting and using indigenous materials rather than those from foreign sources.

Though aware of the Beaux Arts style in Paris, which was

The Tree of Personal Effort – The Sun of Indifference
(1895)
Pencil and watercolour.
13¹¹/₁₆ x 9¹/₄in (32.2 x 23.6cm).

Mackintosh was not entirely happy at Honeyman and Keppie and felt that his talents were neither adequately rewarded nor

even acknowledged: he was simply the anonymous draftsman. This may be the explanation of the symbolism of this watercolour, which was of a style common to The Four. Indeed, it is likely that much of Mackintosh's dissatisfaction was shared by the other three members of the group.

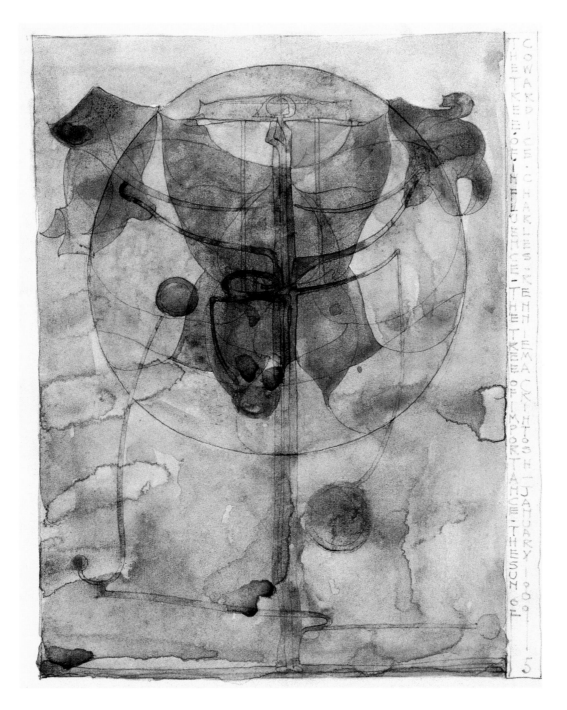

influencing a growing number of young Scottish architects studying in Paris, and of the trend towards neoclassicism, which had long been the mainstay of French and English architects, Mackintosh set out in a new direction, using what he found useful or relevant while searching for a way to express his own personal style.

Mackintosh's early work for Honeyman and Keppie reflected the influence of Italian Renaissance buildings, as required by his employers, and of John James Burnet, the successful Glasgow architect whose predilection for the neo-Renaissance style, with large sloping roofs and doorways with wide architraves, was copied by Mackintosh in early building

The Tree of Influence – The The Tree of Importance – The Sun of Cowardice

In the society of the time, career advancement was in the hands of superiors, who decided who should move up the social ladder and who should not. The son of a police clerk, Mackintosh was less likely to succeed,

and this was clearly what he was expressing in these paintings. The picture opposite indicates his own beliefs, while the picture above symbolizes views to which he was hostile and is undoubtedly a veiled criticism of those who had the power but not the courage to accept new ideas.

LEFT

'The Immortals'

Keppie, McNair and Mackintosh worked on competition drawings at Keppie's Ayrshire home during the week, so relief came at weekends with the arrival of a group of friends from the Glasgow School of Art, among them Jessie Keppie, the Raeburn sisters, Katherine Cameron, Janet Aitken and the Macdonald sisters. They all stayed near the Keppies in two houses in Dunure, north of Culzean, which they called the 'Roaring Camp'. They referred to themselves as 'The Immortals', perhaps not intended to be taken too seriously. These are just some of the group, with Mackintosh himself standing above right.

OPPOSITE ABOVE

From left to right: Katherine Cameron, Charles Rennie Mackintosh, Janet Aitken, John Keppie, Agnes Raeburn, Jessie Keppie, Frances Macdonald, Bertie McNair and Margaret Macdonald.

OPPOSITE RIGHT

Mackintosh and the 'Immortal' girls.

OPPOSITE

The Descent of Night

Watercolour on paper
(1894)

Though this painting
undoubtedly reflects
Mackintosh's state of
mind as he tries to
resolve his emotional and
work problems, it is not
entirely negative. On the
horizon there is a sign of a
pre-dawn glow which
promises that the light of
day will eventually arrive.

LEFT

Summer (Margaret
Macdonald Mackintosh,
1897). Watercolour on
paper.

This is Margaret
Macdonald's contribution
to the output of The Four
as they reach a point in
their lives when they
intend to launch
themselves into individual
careers. At the time,
Margaret and Mackintosh
were about to become
engaged: this is therefore
a somewhat sickly image
of fecundity, and is
unusual in a woman still
some years away from
marriage.

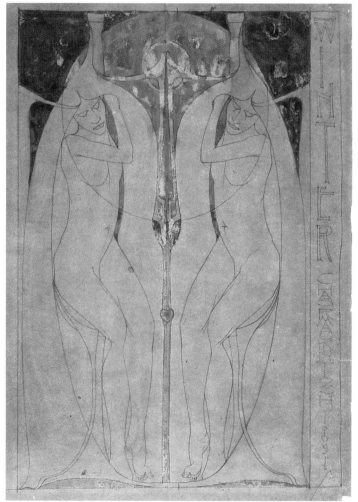

LEFT
Stylized Plant Form (1894)
Watercolour on paper.

A dark and mysterious
atmosphere pervades this
abstruse Mackintosh
rendering of an organic
form. There is growth and
life present, but of a
subterranean kind, possibly
of roots in swampy ground
rather than in full sunlight.
Being a Highland Scot,
Mackintosh was interested
in northern legends and his
work tends to reflect this
dark mythology.

ABOVE
Winter (1895)
Watercolour and pencil.

Though standing, the
female figures appear to
be asleep or in a state of
hibernation, waiting for
spring to arrive, which is
already indicated by the
sprigs of green thrusting
up towards a symbolic
sun. The painting seems
to suggest that winter is
departing and that a
brighter future is soon to
follow.

Competition Entry for the Anglican Cathedral, Liverpool: Perspective
(1902)
Ink and watercolour. 24³/₈ x 36¹/₄ in (61.9 x 92cm).

The high hopes of The Four for the beginning of the century were focused on Mackintosh's entry in a competition for a new Anglican cathedral. Success would mean that

Mackintosh would be accepted as a major architect and would be able to set up on his own. But this was to be the biggest disappointment of Mackintosh's life, for the

project was instead awarded to Giles Gilbert Scott, also the designer of Cambridge University Library and Waterloo Bridge, London.

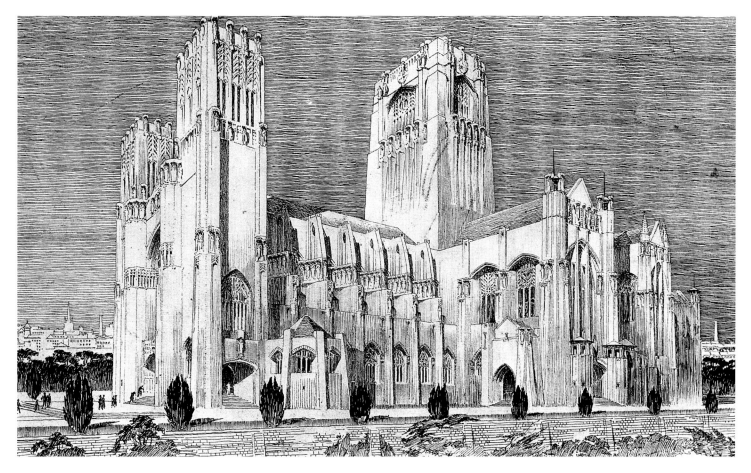

designs. His drawings for the Municipal and Technical Schools in Manchester and the Royal Insurance building in Glasgow bear this out.

Mackintosh's first opportunity to introduce his own individual contribution to a building came in 1893 with the commissioning of Honeyman and Keppie by the *Glasgow Herald* newspaper to design an extension of its premises. Though working within his brief and though he was not credited for his work, Mackintosh's hand is identifiable in the work on the extension's tower, particularly in its asymmetrical windows and organic style of decoration. The *British Architect* magazine remarked on these as being original, if verging on the eccentric, though retaining their architectural quality.

Soon after, in 1895, Mackintosh was engaged on another

Honeyman and Keppie project, this time for the Martyrs' Public School in Glasgow (p. 54–59). In this case, the site for the building was constrained and the budget meagre. The main mass of the building was conventional, therefore, but Mackintosh managed to give it character by including a projecting roof supported by trusses and by disguising the ventilation outlets with three delicate octagonal towers with columns supporting a dome, thus giving an oriental touch to an otherwise conventional brick building.

Other, greater opportunities were soon to arrive for Mackintosh, however. There would be the acceptance of his plans for the Glasgow School of Art in 1896 (p. 38–51), and the interior design of tea rooms, in which the collective flair shown by himself and Margaret Macdonald, whom he married in 1900, would be given full scope (Chapter 5).

ORVIETO.

CRA
1891

OPPOSITE
Orvieto Cathedral, North Elevation (1891)
Pencil and watercolour on paper. (1891)

While on a scholarship tour, funded by the Alexander Thomson Travelling Studentship from March to July 1891, Mackintosh visited many of the important art centres of Italy, including Orvieto, and while there sketched the cathedral, practising his watercolour technique while studying its architecture. The scholarship required that Mackintosh submit examples of work done on his travels, and with this in mind, he concentrated on buildings and ornamentation, leaving little time for visits to art galleries or for studying the Italian masters.

ABOVE
Ill Omen, or Girl in the East Wind with Ravens Passing the Moon
(Frances Macdonald, 1893)
Watercolour and pencil.

Frances Macdonald was a spectator to her sister and Mackintosh's emotional relationship, and shared Mackintosh's feelings concerning the battle of artists striving to influence industrial and commercial society. She also shared the symbolic form of expression of The Four, and married Herbert McNair in 1898. Her *Girl in the East Wind* may be a reference to the situation of women in general, or a personal one expressing her concern for her sister. The ravens, being birds of ill-omen, unknowingly presage the disaster to come.

CHAPTER THREE

FOREIGN GLORY

The saying that a prophet is not without honour, save in his own country, might be said to apply to Charles Rennie Mackintosh. Although enlightened people, such as Francis Newbery, John Davidson, Whynne Bassett-Lowke and Kate Cranston, perceived Mackintosh's original talent, many others did not. Abroad, however, he was quickly recognized as one of a new generation of designer-architects by members of the Secession movement in Germany and Austria.

Secession was the name given to artistic movements in Munich, Dresden and Vienna in which artists had united to break the power of establishment art. Among the leaders of this movement in Vienna were Gustav Klimt, Josef Hoffmann and Kolomon Moser, all of whom admired Mackintosh's work and were influenced by it.

Mackintosh and his friends, Herbert McNair and the Macdonald sisters, had exhibited their work in drawings and watercolours at the London Arts and Crafts Exhibition Society in 1896, but their symbolic drawings had been misunderstood and consequently disliked, earning them the name 'Spook School'.

On the Continent, things were very different, and their work was accepted by all but the most conservative elements still clinging to the academic tradition. To the latter, the work of The Four was an art of hobgoblins and torture chambers. This was very much a rearguard action, for already an article had appeared in the Munich magazine *Dekorative Kunst*, praising the originality of the Glasgow artists and another, by the authoritative critic Hermann Muthesius, was about to appear. Muthesius was soon to become a friend and an enthusiastic supporter of Mackintosh's work. Mackintosh himself knew at first-hand something of the artistic ferment in Europe, having visited Vienna in November 1900.

Encouraged by Muthesius' friendly encouragement, Mackintosh entered a competition organized in 1901 by a German publisher, Alexander Koch of Darmstadt, for a house suitable for art lovers – *Das Haus eines Kunst-Freundes*. Though Mackintosh's drawings were not completed in time to be judged for the prize, the publisher decided to include them in a portfolio which was circulated widely and

The House for an Art Lover (1900–01)

Frustrated by the lack of recognition for his work in Glasgow, the young Mackintosh entered a competition to design a House for an Art Lover, organized by the German publisher of *Zeitschrift für Innendekoration*, Alexander Koch. The house embodied all Mackintosh's novel ideas, especially in its interior, which had a clean-cut sense of space and an originality of decoration that was in startling contrast to the over-furnished houses of the time. Although the house was not built, the publisher produced a portfolio of Mackintosh's drawings which had a wide circulation and influence on a new generation of architects in Europe. The house was finally built in 1988 at Bellahouston Park in Glasgow, after Mackintosh's original designs had been augmented by Andy Macmillan, then head of the Mackintosh School of Architecture in Glasgow. A copy of it was erected in Japan.

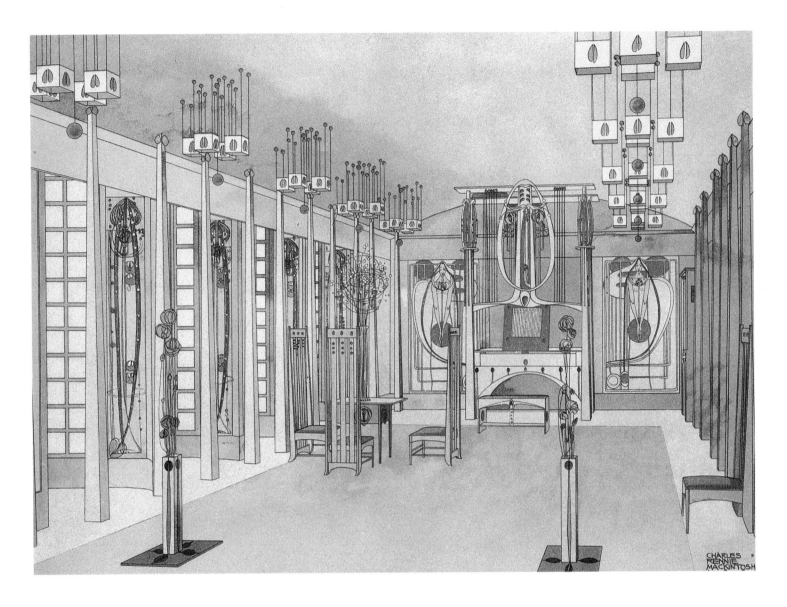

helped to further establish Mackintosh as a leading designer and architect. Mackintosh's drawings not only included the exterior of the house, but also detailed interiors in a style which was soon to appear in other work he was undertaking. The house itself, though soon familiar to everyone interested in architecture through reproductions of plans and drawings, was not built until 1988 when it was erected in Glasgow's Bellahouston Park, where it now houses the Glasgow School of Art post-graduate department.

Writing about the portfolio drawings, Hermann Muthesius commented, 'The exterior architecture of the building evinces an absolutely original character unlike anything else known.' An examination of the portfolio confirms his views and shows that the interior planned by Mackintosh was even more original and daring.

The following year, Mackintosh was invited by Francis Newbery to exhibit at the International Exhibition of

The House for an Art Lover (1900–01)

ABOVE is a view of the salon and music room, part of the original design for the competition, which consists of a perspective view and three wall elevations.

OPPOSITE ABOVE is a faithful reconstruction of Mackintosh's original design which was completed in the 1980s by architects John Kane and Graeme Robertson.

RIGHT
This is the original
Mackintosh design for the
dining room, featuring an
abundance of panelling
inset with stained glass,
built-in furniture, and his
trademark high-backed
chairs.

The House for an Art Lover

Here is the 1980s dining room, an accurate representation taken from Mackintosh's original competition drawing from 1900–01 (see previous page).

The House for an Art Lover

View of the hall, looking through to the dining room.

Modern Decorative Art in Turin, the home of the Italian royal family in Piedmont and soon to become the famous capital of the Italian motor car industry. Newbery saw this as an opportunity to increase the European reputation of his star students and encouraged Mackintosh and his wife, Margaret, to participate.

The space devoted to the Scottish exhibitors turned out to be disappointing. It was a long narrow corridor with recesses and little atmosphere, but Mackintosh and Margaret immediately set to work to make long Art Nouveau banners at each intersection, imparting a sense of unity to the whole space. Their main exhibit was a boudoir with, naturally

enough, a feminine theme; the walls were painted in pale colours, giving the room a light and airy feel, but which led an Italian critic to describe it as puritanical and functional, which was hardly surprising in a country where houses were cluttered with heavy furniture inherited from ancestors.

The Mackintoshes furnished the room with high-backed chairs with stencilled decorations and inlaid glass, and Margaret hung two large gesso panels on the end walls. There was also a mirror.

As elsewhere, the Mackintoshs' spare approach created interest and began to influence local taste. Their influence, however, was strongest in Vienna, home of the Secession.

OPPOSITE

The Rose Boudoir

(International Exhibition of Modern Decorative Art, Turin, 1902)

This room design is simple and made the most of the space available, in complete contrast to the prevailing style and which Italian critics considered to be too spartan. The decorations included gesso panels by Margaret Mackintosh, using several techniques, and other three-dimensional decorative features.

They were now asked to design a music room for the Wärndofers, who were financial backers of the Vienna Secession artists and enthusiasts of the modern style.

Here, too, Mackintosh chose a light and airy style with walls in pale colours with touches of lavender and rose. The walls were decorated with gesso panels by both Mackintosh and Margaret, the theme for which was taken from *Seven Princesses*, a work by the Belgian dramatist and follower of the Symbolist movement, Maurice Maeterlinck. Margaret also painted two panels entitled *The Opera of the Sea*, which were set into the piano. A charming feature of the room were two alcoves either side of the fireplace, each containing high-backed chairs.

Following this was a visit to Moscow at the invitation of the Grand Duke Serge, then a further invitation by the Dresdener Werkstätten für Handwerkskunst, for which Mackintosh designed a bedroom setting, the twin beds set in a recess, with two pillars of shelving on either side. The bedheads were decorated with pendants and the bed ends were square and plain. The whole effect was of intimacy and space and reflected the way in which Charles and Margaret Mackintosh collaborated with one another in this the most creative period of their early married life.

The White Rose and the Red Rose (1902)
Painted gesso panel on hessian, set with string, glass beads and shell. 39 x 40in (99 x 101.5cm).

Designed by Margaret Macdonald Mackintosh for the Rose Boudoir, Turin Exhibition.

CHAPTER FOUR
THE PUBLIC BUILDINGS

The Glasgow School of Art (1897–1909)

RIGHT
Mackintosh designed this door plaque for the main entrance to the Glasgow School of Art, which is the focus for the highly dramatic flight of stairs which narrows towards the top, leading through the double doors and into the vaulted entrance hall, up the main staircase, and to the director's office above (p. 44–45).

OPPOSITE
A competition held in 1896 for a design for a new building to house the Glasgow School of Art was won by Mackintosh. The first phase (1897–99) terminated at the main entrance tower of the north elevation, while the splendid west side, OPPOSITE, with its strong verticals and projecting bays, was designed to house the magnificent two-storey library, and took from 1907 to 1909 to complete.

Glasgow's importance as a centre of industry and design had created an international demand for art education, which the corporation galleries were unable to meet. This encouraged Francis Newbery, the principal of the school, to approach the board of governors of the Glasgow School of Art with a proposal to raise funds for a new building in which it would be housed. The board liked the idea, and the project was put out to tender to eight Glasgow architectural practices, including John Honeyman and Keppie, who were awarded the contract on the basis of designs by Charles Rennie Mackintosh.

Mackintosh was entrusted with the entire project, and produced what is generally regarded as an architectural masterpiece which, while linked to the traditional, was also highly original, ahead of its time, and in line with work seen in Brussels and Paris by Horta and Guimard, in America by Frank Lloyd Wright, and in Barcelona by Antoní Gaudí, all of them pioneers of Modernism.

Mackintosh was aware of modernist efforts to break with established formulae, but also had a good understanding of the architectural heritage of Western art, through his study of Medieval, Renaissance, Byzantine and Gothic forms, and of the vernacular architecture of Scotland and the work of C.F.A.Voysey of the English Free School. As a Glaswegian living in one of the most industrially advanced cities in the world, he was well aware of the new technologies available for working with steel, timber, plate glass and other materials. In his plans for the Glasgow School of Art he took all these into account, while keeping firmly to the idea that a building was an organic entity with its own *raison d'être* which had to be respected and not simply as an idea on a drawing board.

The first stage of construction, which continued until 1899, began in 1897. The main entrance to this part of the building, on the north side in Renfrew Street, was given an asymmetrical design, with the entrance doorway, reached by a flight of stairs, set in a recessed, stepped framework and with

THE GLASGOW SCHOOL of ART
PLANS OF NEW SCHOOL

EAST
ELEVATION

WEST
ELEVATION

The Glasgow School of Art

Plans were completed in March 1897 for the new school of art, showing the east and west elevations and a cross-section through the library.

a large bay with square panes on its east wall. Above the doorway, another window gave light to the director's room, while above and to the left was an oriole window which lit the stairs to the studios. These were later added to and extended along the whole of the new west wing, added from 1907–09.

When the building was completed, the centre entrance section was flanked by plain walls with large windows to provide maximum natural lighting for the studios. These windows were varied by being given different numbers of panes on the east and west ends of the façade and each window was given a supporting curved iron bracket with an

N°6

SECTION
THROUGH
LIBRARY

140 BATH STREET
GLASGOW. MARCH 97

ornamental head and a projection, originally intended as a support for planks on which a window cleaner could stand.

Later, in the second stage, the west façade, Mackintosh introduced long bay windows to give maximum light to the library; instead of being inserted in the wall, as on the Renfrew Street front, these protruded in elegant bays supported by the stonework above and below. The effect was both modern and practical, and embodied the principles of architecture to which Mackintosh subscribed. There was no trace of neoclassicism.

The interiors were as original as the exterior. The library,

Glasgow School of Art

The motif of the glass panels on the doors of the entrance to Studio 45 suggests Margaret Macdonald's fine feminine hand. The stylized roses, supported by several vertical stems, was a theme that both she and

Mackintosh adopted and had both a spiritual and sexual symbolism.

The Glasgow School of Art

OPPOSITE
The west façade relates closely to the structure of the library within and displays Mackintosh's architectural genius to the full. Its exaggerated grids and verticals gave rise to surprisingly little comment at the time.

ABOVE
The modern technology available in industrial Glasgow meant that all the clocks in the Glasgow School of Art could be synchronized with a central master clock. Though Mackintosh was open to modern techniques he avoided uniformity by giving each clock face its own individual character.

The Glasgow School of Art

LEFT and ABOVE
The main north entrance of the Glasgow School of Art in Renfew Street was designed by Mackintosh to be something of an asymmetrical tour de force. A square lamp hangs above the arch which leads up a narrowing flight of stairs to the double doors at the top. The entire front is a series of architectural masses balanced one against the other and quite different from the symmetrical geometry of classical buildings. Above the entrance doors was the office of the director, Francis Newbery, who encouraged his talented students, known as The Four. Mackintosh designed the door plaque especially for him.

The Glasgow School of Art

OPPOSITE
The east façade is full of variety and invention. The main group of windows are surmounted by a semi-circular arch which is recessed, and the tall, narrow windows with latticed panes provide a witty contrast in a satisfying total design.

LEFT and BELOW
The use of wrought-iron brackets on the north façade windows were for the purpose of strengthening them. However, this entirely practical use of the material has become a famous feature of this great landmark and gives the building a workmanlike quality which is reflected in the building's function as an art school.

The Glasgow School of Art

ABOVE
Roof arch seen from the west.

OPPOSITE
The masterpiece of the second floor of the building is the library, an astonishingly modern concept for its time when libraries were musty vaults furnished with heavy wooden bookcases and solid desks. Mackintosh gave his library tall dark columns the full height of the two-storeyed room, and pendent lights hanging from the ceiling with shades resembling stylized flowers. Daylight enters through the tall slender windows which run the full height of the room.

with its height running to two storeys, provided air and space and was lit by octagonal hanging lights, whose long vertical cables echoed the powerful dark beams that soared to the ceiling from the polished wooden floor.

Another storey was added in a later stage of the building, with a director's room, a loggia and a long covered glass passageway, originally as a link between the male and female divisions of the school.

The Glasgow School of Art was undoubtedly Mackintosh's masterpiece of public building and established his reputation not only as an architect but also as a designer; the furniture and artefacts were designed by him and, no doubt, by his wife Margaret, who collaborated closely with him throughout their lives together.

While working on the Glasgow School of Art, Mackintosh was also engaged in designs for the Queen's Cross Church (p. 64–69), the only ecclesiastical building of his architectural career, apart for his rejected plans for Liverpool's Anglican Cathedral. The church, which expresses

The Glasgow School of Art

The boardroom was completed by Mackintosh in 1906 and is a formal room lit by three sets of nine lamps in copper shades, and adorned with carved wooden pilasters (see opposite).

ABOVE
Panelling and pilasters can often be seen in boardrooms and other formal rooms. Here Mackintosh has used a classical Greek temple theme to decorate this pilaster in the school's boardroom. The other detailing bears all the hallmarks of Mackintosh's original work.

ABOVE RIGHT
This finial, with its perching bird, is a charming addition to the Glasgow School of Art, where it is placed high on the roof over the main entrance, and confirms Mackintosh's keen eye for detail and management of the total design.

the ideas on mass and weight which Mackintosh believed to be essential in architecture, is also surprisingly modern in its interior, where strong roof ties impart a sense of space as well as strength.

Despite his early success with the Martyrs' School (p. 54–59), and the acclaim of his work by European architects and designers, Mackintosh was hardly inundated with commissions for large public buildings and was not approached for a large project until 1903, when he was commissioned by the Govan School Board in Glasgow to build a school in Scotland Street (p. 60–63) .

The Scotland Street School was, apart for the completion of the Glasgow School of Art, his last large public building, which makes it all the more unfortunate that he was limited in his plans by a small budget, which precluded the building of anything apart from the basic structure. Despite the financial constraint, however, Mackintosh created a modern school full of character. He accommodated the building's two main stairwells in towers with elongated rectangular windows which, seen from outside, gave the towers an impression of height and provided plenty of natural light in the interior, an innovation later used by Walter Gropius in his stairwells for a factory and offices in Cologne in 1914.

The Lady Artists' Club
(1908)

THIS PAGE and OPPOSITE
The doorway of this house in Blythswood Square, Glasgow, with its semi-circular arch, contrasts dramatically with the triangular pediment and, backed by a lattice-work design of window panes, is typical of the products of Mackintosh's fertile imagination. His impeccable sense of mass and space came from a natural inclination to avoid geometrical symmetry and to seek architectural diversity.

Perspective Drawing of The Martyrs' Public School, Glasgow

(1895–98)

Ink on paper. 24$^{1}/_{8}$ x 36$^{7}/_{8}$in (61.3 x 92.7cm).

This is Charles Rennie Mackintosh's own drawing of his first building, in which a standard School Board plan was utilized for the building with segregated entrances and stairs at each end.

The Martyrs' School

OPPOSITE and ABOVE
The red-brick school was
one of Mackintosh's first
jobs for Honeyman and
Keppie. Despite the
awkward location and

restricted budget, he
designed a building with
unexpected points of
interest, such as the
overhanging roof and the
Japanese pagoda-like
towers which conceal the
ventilation system.

57

The Martyrs' School

There was a little more scope for Mackintosh's ingenuity in the interior of the building, where he turned the stairwell into a handsome space defined by the dark verticals and horizontals of banisters and stair rails. Across the skylight through which daylight illuminated the stairs, he placed arched beams enhanced with a decorative design.

ABOVE and BELOW
The roof trusses used in
the Martyrs' School are
similar to those to be seen
in the Glasgow School of
Art and in the Queen's
Cross Church.

ABOVE RIGHT
The detailing around the
ceilings, and the use of
tiles and wrought iron, are
echoed in many others of
Mackintosh's works.

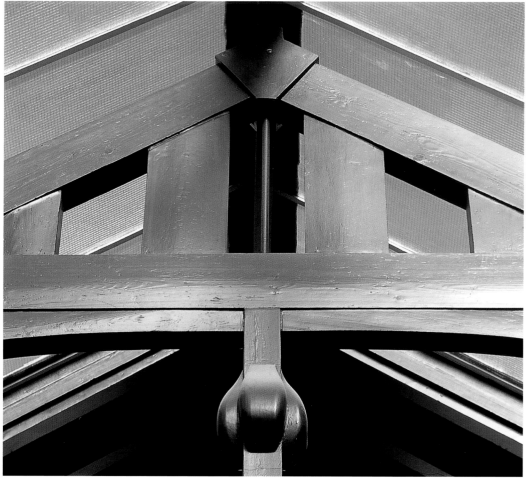

Scotland Street School, Glasgow (1903–04)

The school should have been in white stone, but Mackintosh was overruled by the School Board on grounds of tradition and expense. Despite these constraints, he produced a highly original building whose cylindrical stairwells influenced the work of Walter Gropius at Cologne. The horizontal bands of windows and the decorations of small squares of coloured tiles, make a strong contrast to the rounded forms of the stairwell towers.

Scotland Street School

FAR LEFT
This was Mackintosh's last major and completely new work in Glasgow. The stair towers are truly extraordinary and just as breathtaking from the outside as the inside.

LEFT
The school was built with three storeys of classrooms and a mezzanine containing other accommodations, such as cloakrooms. While the school was built to comply with standards set by the Scottish Department of Education, it still managed to retain all the intrinsic flair of Mackintosh's original design.

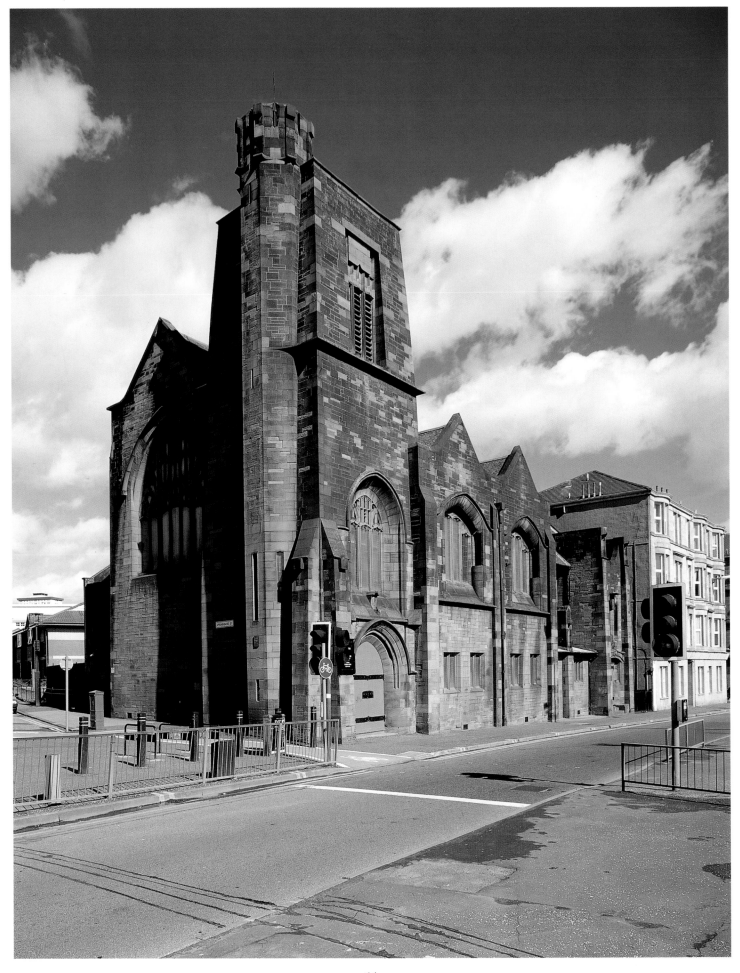

St MATTHEWS CHURCH GLASGOW

: NOW QUEEN'S CROSS CHURCH :

CHARLES·R·MACKINTOSH·F.R.I.B.A

JOHN HONEYMAN AND KEPPIE
ARCHITECTS :
140 BATH STREET : GLASGOW.

OPPOSITE

Queen's Cross Church

(1897–99)

When he was
commissioned to design
St Matthew's Church at
Queen's Cross,
Mackintosh was able to
carry out some of the
ideas concerning the unity

of a building that he had
formulated through his
contact with the
Secessionists in Vienna.
Within a conventional
format he was able to give
the building a particular
character by his disposition
of its masses and in the
interior by his manipulation
of spatial proportions.

ABOVE

**Perspective Architectural
Drawing for the Queen's
Cross Church**

Ink on paper.

Queen's Cross Church

LEFT
The Art Nouveau influence is visible on the detail of the design on the pulpit, repeated five times around its curving façade. The long sinuous curves of a plant form are enclosed by what is possibly a dove's wing, symbolizing the Holy Spirit.

RIGHT, ABOVE and BELOW
At first sight, this Gothic-style window may appear to be like any other in a Scottish church. However, the vibrant stained glass within is just as effectively echoed in the delicate tracery without, and demonstrates how masterfully Mackintosh was able to combine his architecture and artwork into a satisfying whole.

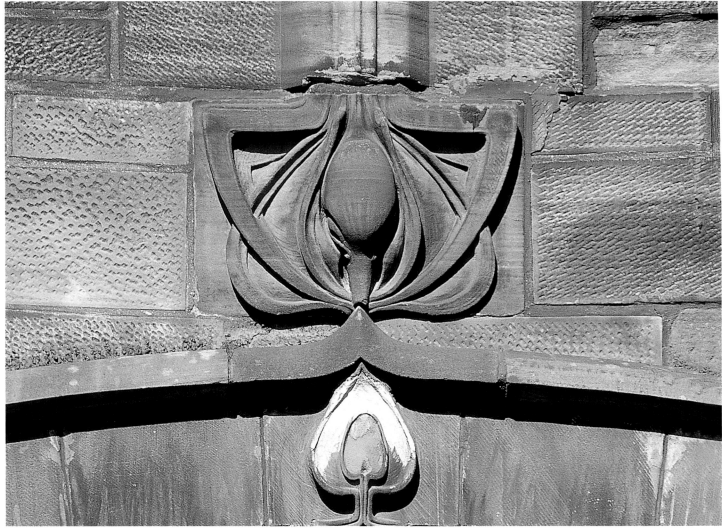

Queen's Cross Church
OPPOSITE, ABOVE and
BELOW

Again, at first glance, the
Queen's Cross Church may
appear conventional, but
closer inspection reveals
that Mackintosh has
adopted a modern-Gothic
symbolism, while providing
the required degree of
spirituality necessary in a
place of worship.

RIGHT
The design on the back of
the pulpit (p. 66) is striking
in its beautiful curves and
forms.

BELOW RIGHT
The Communion Table,
with its delicately arched
forms, measures $28^{7}/_{16}$ x
60 x $26^{11}/_{16}$in (72.5 x 152.4
x 67.8cm) and was made
by Francis Smith.

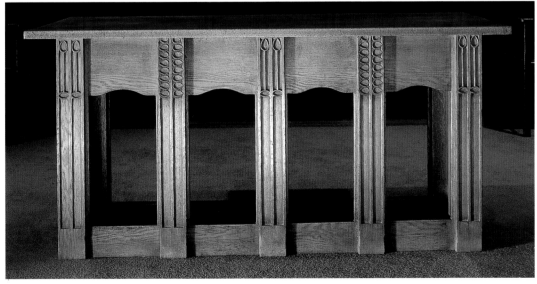

CHAPTER FIVE

ART NOUVEAU &
TEA ROOMS

Catherine Cranston

Kate Cranston virtually invented the Glasgow tea room, in that she recognized the need for meeting places, not only for men but also and more importantly for women, who could meet there without chaperones. (This was at a time when a lone woman would be taken for

Tea rooms may lack the grandeur of public buildings but like textiles, furniture and objets d'art they are a medium through which the fundamental principles of art can be expressed and become influential in other fields. This was the case with Mackintosh's tea rooms which became, perhaps to his own surprise, models of originality in his time and continued to influence architects and designers into the 20th century.

Mackintosh's first encounter with the genre was in 1896, when Kate Cranston, the wife of a tea importer, asked him to create stencil decorations for her newly-built tea room in Buchanan Street, having no doubt seen some of the watercolours and screens exhibited by The Four.

a servant or a prostitute.) They were not cafés in the modern sense of the word, but a selection of meeting rooms, with spaces for reading and writing, and of course places to smoke and play billiards. They almost had the status of a club, but were without bedrooms and, most importantly of all, without alcohol.

The Willow Tea Room

(1903)

Mackintosh had been commissioned to decorate or provide furniture for Kate Cranston tea rooms in Buchanan Street in 1896, Argyle Street in 1898 and Ingram Street in 1900, so by 1903 she was eager for him to remodel a building in Sauchiehall Street which was to become yet another tea room. Mackintosh began with the front, stripping away the existing mouldings to construct a façade of shallow curves and deeply recessed upper windows, with an elegant first-floor window with narrow vertical columns across almost the entire width of the building. The ground floor was set back to create a recessed space, making the entrance more removed from its neighbours but nonetheless welcoming. The top floor was reserved for men's smoking and billiard rooms.

Kate Cranston's husband, Stuart, had already opened a number of tea rooms in order to promote sales of his tea, which were simple places with no other object in view than to provide a place for working men to enjoy a cup of tea or a simple lunch. In fact, tea rooms found many of their customers among temperance supporters, of whom there were a growing number in a city renowned for hard drinking.

Kate Cranston, evidently a determined woman with a flair for business, decided to improve on the existing tea rooms by serving teas in more attractive premises which would cater for men, women and families. She bought premises in Buchanan Street and Argyle Street in an area frequented by shoppers and within reach of the business quarter south of George Square.

These premises were specially designed for her by George Washington Brown and the decorations installed by George Walton. Mackintosh provided hanging stencilled wall decorations for the Buchanan Street premises, but undertook all the interior design and furniture for Argyle Street, where Walton did the wall decorations.

In line with other establishments, Kate Cranston tea rooms served light lunches as well as tea and also included smoking and billiard rooms for men. The pleasant ambience of her tea rooms soon attracted attention and drew in more customers, and Mackintosh's work evidently pleased Mrs Cranston, for she now offered him sole responsibility for the design of yet another tea room, this time in Ingram Street.

The Ingram Street building was a larger project for which Mackintosh built a series of tea rooms. His work began in 1900 when Kate asked him to totally redesign the existing interior, which had a wide frontage extending from numbers 205 to 215. Given a free hand and unhampered by a framework of another architect's work, he began by gutting the entire interior and redesigning the space in a series of interconnecting rooms.

The main space on the ground floor was the White Luncheon Room, which was lit by huge windows through which the daylight filtered onto white tablecloths laid with cutlery designed by Mackintosh. Also on the ground floor were a Chinese Room, which was built in 1911, the Ladies'

The Willow Tea Room

OPPOSITE and ABOVE
The first-floor window is
one of the Willow Tea
Room's most distinctive
features, and has
contributed to making it the
most famous of all the
establishments. The
windows bear Art Nouveau
motifs, finding their echo in
the Salon de Luxe inside.

RIGHT
Mackintosh's square-faced
clock in its latticed case
seems rather severe until
one examines the elegant
numbers on the dial, which

suggest the influence on
Mackintosh of Viennese
Art Nouveau styles. The
original clock was made for
the Willow Tea Room and
a later copy was made for
Berlin, and it is not known
where it actually stood.
However, the clock's dark
colour and masculine
appearance suggests that
it may have been intended
for a men's smoking or
billiard room.

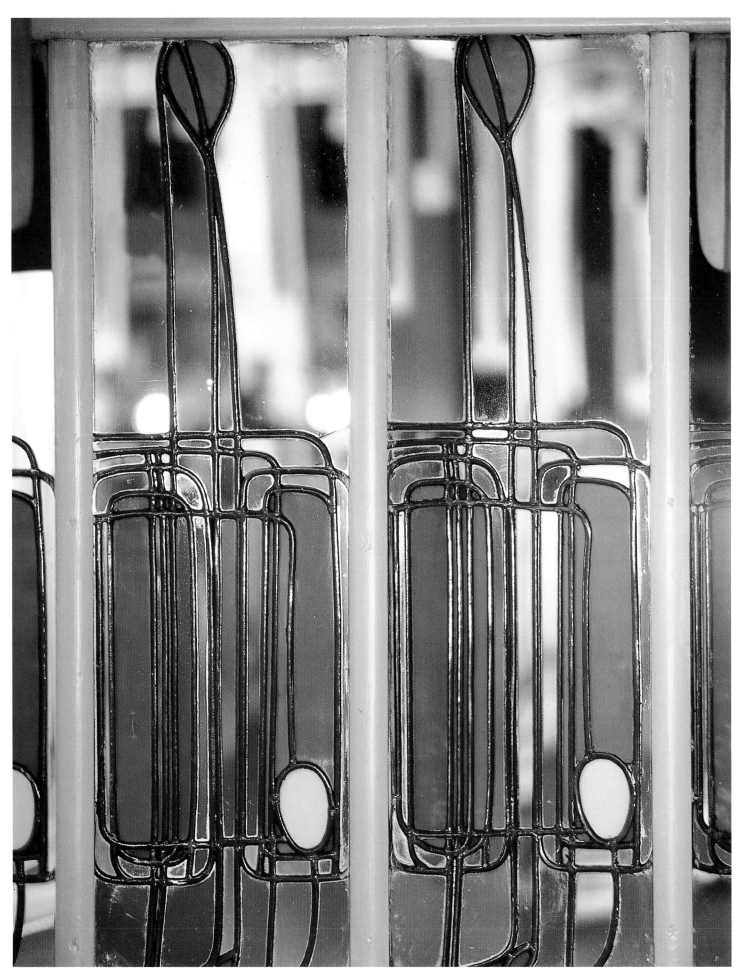

The Willow Tea Room

OPPOSITE and RIGHT
The Salon de Luxe, behind the first-floor façade, was the most extravagant of the Mackintosh tea room designs. The intricate details of the panels were extended even to the cutlery, fulfilling Mackintosh's theories on the need for complete artistic co-ordination. The room has a feminine appearance, the high-backed chairs affording privacy without obscuring the view.

BELOW
This settle was for the Dug-Out, a 1916 basement extension to the tea room.

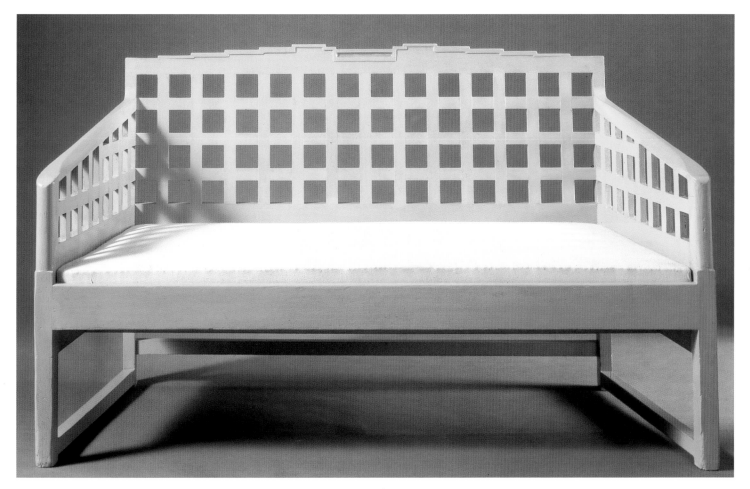

The Willow Tea Room

LEFT
The Gallery.

BELOW
This photograph of the Salon De Luxe shows how finely the intricate glass panels and entrance door have been made to harmonize with the furniture and flooring.

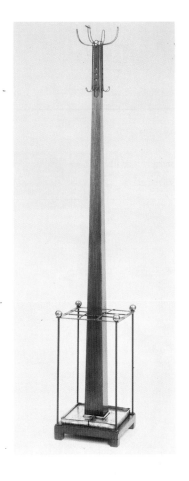

The Ingram Street Tea Room (1900)

OPPOSITE ABOVE RIGHT
Hat, coat and umbrella stand for the White Luncheon Room.

ABOVE
Oak chair for the White Luncheon Room.

Luncheon Room, a darker-toned Oak Room, and a barrel-vaulted Cloister Room, added a little later. The Luncheon Room, Ladies' Luncheon Room and Oak Room were part of a galleried section on the first floor which, after the building was demolished in 1963, were reconstructed at the Glasgow Museum. All the rooms had their own furniture designed by Mackintosh, which varied from the solid barrel armchairs of the masculine domains to the delicate rectilinear chairs of the Chinese Room which made considerable use of white lattice-work screens.

Of all the tea rooms which Mackintosh designed there is no doubt that the Willow Tea Room, situated among Glasgow's newest shops and department stores in Sauchiehall Street, was the most finished example of his oeuvre, as well as marking a change in his collaboration with his wife Margaret.

In 1903, Mackintosh began work on the Willow Tea Room, named for its location, 'sauchiehall' being derived from the Celtic and meaning 'a boggy place full of willows'.

The building was four storeys high and was of similar size to the Ingram Street building. Mackintosh began with the exterior from which he removed all the surface mouldings, giving half of it an undulating curve with windows buried in

ABOVE
Oak chair designed for the Chinese Room of the Ingram Street tea room, which Mackintosh redesigned in 1911, the Chinese element coming from the predominance of lattice and fretwork screens placed against canvas wall-coverings painted a powerful blue.

LEFT
Tea room waitresses

BELOW LEFT
The Willow Tea Room
A settle designed in 1904.

RIGHT
The Argyle Street Tea Room (1898)
Chair.

the façade and a ground-floor entrance recessed below a long rectangular window.

Mackintosh organized the Willow Tea Room interior as he had at Ingram Street, allowing sight lines from one area to another and creating a sense of space. This was a new concept in architecture, regarded by the architectural historian Nikolaus Pevsner as equal to the work of Frank Lloyd Wright in America and Le Corbusier in Europe. The tea room on the ground floor opened up to a rear luncheon room and stairs led up to a tea gallery. Above this was the Salon de Luxe, an elegant room with pale furniture and high-backed chairs which afforded privacy without making the room look crowded and heavy with furniture.

All the decorations were undoubtedly the result of a collaboration with Margaret, and some work was entirely of her design. This was the last time her delicate handiwork would be detected, for after the Willow Tea Room Mackintosh's work became decidedly more sombre and masculine.

By the time his last contribution to the Willow Tea Room had been made in 1911, Mackintosh was becoming increasingly depressed at the lack, not only of large architectural commissions coming his way, but also the paucity of interest in Britain concerning his designs. He had begun to drink heavily and a sad period in his life began, casting a heavy cloud on his marriage.

BELOW

The Buchanan Street Tea Room (1897)

Preliminary design for a mural decoration for the first-floor tea room.

ABOVE LEFT
Ebonized clock with inlaid decoration
(c.1917)

ABOVE
Tall-backed chair

LEFT
Mahogany table with mother-of-pearl inlay
(1918)

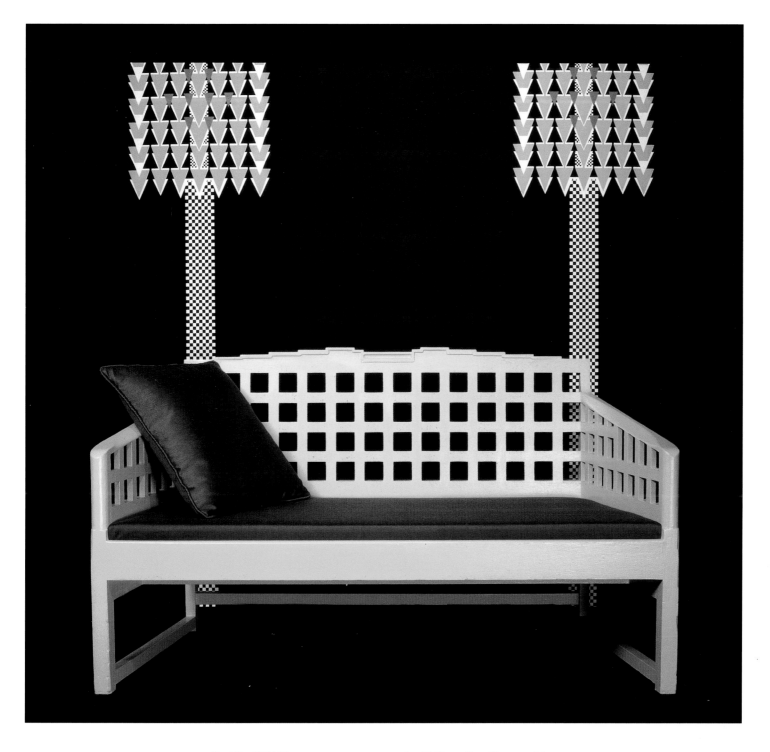

Settle (1916)

Dimensions: 31¼ x 54 x 27¾in (79.4 x 137 x 70.5cm).

Constructed of wood, painted yellow. Designed for the Dug-Out, the basement extension to the Willow Tea Room, this is another view of the settle on page 75, but is seen here against an interesting background, no doubt the later work of Charles Rennie Mackintosh.

CHAPTER SIX

HOUSES TO LIVE IN

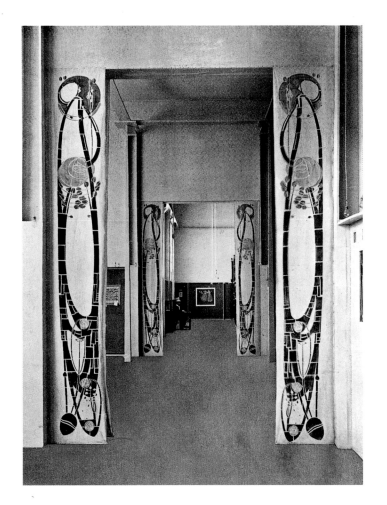

ABOVE

International Exhibition of Modern Decorative Art, Turin (1902)

Entrance to the exhibition. Mackintosh designed the installation for the Scottish section, which included a room setting, the Rose Boudoir, (p. 36 and 37) by Mackintosh in collaboration with Margaret Macdonald.

Mackintosh's success with interior design, possibly enhanced by his happy partnership with Margaret, for a time deflected his interest in public building and directed it towards domestic architecture, in which a house was to be regarded as a unified concept.

This was an idea proposed and promoted by the Vienna Secessionists with whom Mackintosh was beginning to find accord. Josef Hoffmann, one of the pioneers of the Viennese group, had an uncompromising belief that every aspect of a dwelling should conform to a single theme (as in the Stoclet Palace, Brussels), down to details like cutlery and napkins. During his visit to Vienna in 1900, Mackintosh had absorbed many of these radical views though, with his strong Scottish individualism, he was unable to fully accept the subjugation of every part to the whole. To him a house was not, in the catchword of later years, 'a machine for living in', but an expression of a shared life with room for individual tastes.

ABOVE and OPPOSITE

The Eighth Vienna Secession Exhibition (1900)

The Four collaborated to produce exhibits which did not appeal to the Viennese critics. However, Mackintosh benefited from seeing other progressive exhibits which provided inspiration for his later work. Above is a cabinet and chair, while opposite is a detail from the Scottish Room.

Putting this into practice, the Mackintoshes began by remodelling their first home, a flat at 120 Mains Street, with rooms that had either a male or female character, the former with a dark ambience and the latter possessing a light and airy quality. The dining room was given a dark, strong decor and was furnished with a sturdy table and high-backed chairs with oval headpieces, while the walls were covered with brown paper.

The bedroom had a light decor with pale walls and carpet and a large window, before which stood a mirror, and the drawing room, sparsely furnished, had two large windows which provided ample illumination for the light furniture. To most people, accustomed to drawing rooms crowded with opulent sofas, over-stuffed armchairs and assorted bric à brac, the clean lines and sense of space of the Mackintoshes' flat must have seemed spartan in its severity. On the top floor the Mackintoshes had a studio, another rather spare room, with a

fireplace surround of 14 roughly-hewn white planks which provided a dramatic contrast to the dark high-backed chair standing before it. Their experiments in the flat served them well when they began to work on the tea rooms that Kate Cranston was beginning to commission.

In 1906, theMackintoshes moved to a house in Florentine Terrace. Here they became more adventurous, producing a balanced scheme of rooms and spaces which had a decidedly Japanese feeling. The narrow entrance hall was kept dark in tone but had two mirrors and was treated as an antechamber to the rest of the house. A dining room (p. 86), also on the ground floor, was similarly muted in character with a strong simple table and high-backed dark chairs in a room with panelled walls up to a height of 6ft (1.8m) under a light ceiling.

Upstairs the house was a realm of light and space. The drawing room, in contrast to the floor below, sparkled with

The Mackintosh House

The house, formerly at 6, Florentine Terrace, has been reconstructed in the Hunterian Art Gallery, University of Glasgow, using the original furniture light from two windows and flowed across the pale carpet on which stood some of the furniture from their former home. The bedroom, also in pale colours, had a curious box-like four-poster-type bed with two large apertures at the foot and a decorative tapestry at the head.

The studio space (p. 88–89) was the most remarkable of all, with its shoulder-height cupboards with black-and-white designs of trees, and an imposing desk which, with its doors open, looked like the silhouette of a Japanese kimono and was similar to the one designed for Hill House. The house was demolished in 1963 but fortunately some of it was reconstructed at the Hunterian Art Gallery where the Mackintoshes' congenial interior remains to be enjoyed by the present-day visitors, who are more in tune with and fitments. ABOVE is a beaten-silver panel by Margaret Macdonald Mackintosh, dating from 1899, and made for the fireplace of the Mains Street bedroom.

The Mackintosh House

When the Mackintoshes married in 1900 they moved into a flat in Mains Street, Glasgow and began to decorate it in the style that they both believed to be suitable for a world which was becoming more industrialized and streamlined. Their rooms

Mackintosh's originality than were most of his contemporaries.

While working on his first home at Mains Street, Mackintosh was asked by a relative, William Davidson, to design for him a house, Windyhill, at Kilmacolm (p. 90–93). It was Mackintosh's first design for a detached house and he based it on a Scottish farmhouse, with steeply pitched roofs and rough grey-cladded walls. The interior was also based on traditional lines but modified with Mackintosh's own innovations. In the hall, for instance, the fireplace is framed in a slim arch reminiscent of an entrance arch, a Torii gate to a Shinto shrine. With such details Mackintosh began to introduce modern ideas into conventional surroundings.

In 1901 Mackintosh was given the opportunity to create

were designed to be bright, airy and spacious and their furniture light and finely crafted. ABOVE is the studio-drawing room, looking south-east, which has a distinctive quality of clarity and calm and is the very antithesis of the sombre, cluttered interiors prevalent at the time.

The Mackintosh House

The dining room was previously in the Mackintoshes' Mains Street apartment, and when they bought their new house in Florentine Terrace in 1906 they

an interior completely to his own design. This was at Kingsborough Gardens, the home of the Rowats who were related to the Newbery family. The interior decorations were executed in pale colours and with a feminine character that suggest the hand of Margaret Mackintosh. The drawing room, in particular, with its long white fireplace and corner settle with seven decorated panels, was elegantly modern, causing Hermann Muthesius to remark in *Das Englisches Haus*, 'Mackintosh interiors achieve a level of sophistication which is beyond the lives of even the most artistically educated of the population. The refinement and austerity of the artistic atmosphere prevailing here does not reflect the ordinariness that fills so much of our lives.'

In fact, Mackintosh's taste was far in advance, even of

rebuilt it there. The dining room incorporates a striking set of high-backed chairs which were the first Mackintosh designed. The room is in dark tones, broken by splashes of a lighter colour.

ABOVE
The cheval mirror for the
bedroom dates from 1900,
and was originally in the
Mains Street apartment.

those who prided themselves on keeping up with the times.
For them, modernity meant the plushy backgrounds of the
portraits of John Singer Sargent and the elegance of salons
mimicking the grandeur of Louis XIV palaces. Such people
found the spare, airy rectilinear interiors devised by
Mackintosh difficult to accept. Fortunately for Mackintosh,
there were some who understood what he was trying to
achieve, and one of these was Walter Blackie, the publisher.

Blackie had heard of Mackintosh through Talwin Morris,
an artist friend of Newbery, and had become interested in
seeing his work. He therefore asked William Davidson's
permission to visit Windyhill and was sufficiently impressed to
discuss his own plans with Mackintosh. By good fortune, for
Mackintosh was not inclined to yield where his own designs

ABOVE
This chair, dating from
1902, is made of oak
painted white, with glass
insets, stencilled fabric
back and silk seat. It was
originally designed for the
Rose Boudoir room (p. 36
and 37), exhibited at Turin
that same year.

The Mackintosh House

The studio-drawing room has shoulder-height bookcases with black-and-white tree shapes, and a kimono-like desk, which saw its beginnings in a similar one designed for The Hill House (p. 103).

were concerned, they both agreed on almost all aspects of the house required by Blackie, and out of this emerged one of Mackintosh's most felicitous domestic buildings.

The land on which The Hill House (p. 94–103) was to be built overlooked the Clyde at Helensburgh, in a fine residential area, and was a site guaranteed to stir Mackintosh's imagination. He had recently been commended in Vienna for a plan for a House for an Art Lover, and here was an opportunity for some of these ideas to be brought to fruition (see p. 28–35). However, with his strong sense of location and

Windyhill, Kilmacolm
(1900)

Windyhill was completed in 1901 for a relative, William Davidson, and was Mackintosh's first detached house for a middle-class client. The furniture was very much in the Arts and Crafts style and the stylized rose on the glass panel of this bookcase came to be regarded as a hallmark of the collaboration of Mackintosh and his wife, Margaret Macdonald, and symbolized their close relationship. The curves and straight lines of the design create a perfect balance and convey the significance of their relationship at the most creative period of their lives together.

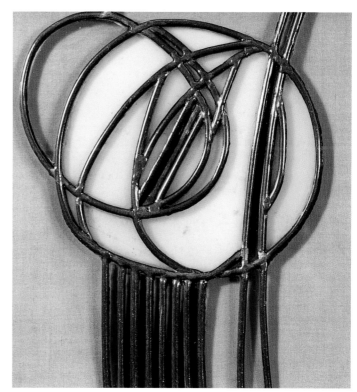

his Highland background, he gave the exterior an appearance derived from Scottish vernacular architecture. Like most sensitive artists he was aware that new must come out of old and that cultural continuity must be preserved.

It was one of Mackintosh's strengths in all his work that he recognized the demands of particular environments and the utilitarian needs of the spaces he designed. He was not a theorist who applied a formula to projects, as with some later architects, but treated all the parts of a buildings as a cohesive whole, while retaining their individual character.

Thus in Hill House he allowed the exterior to be dictated by the character of the interior spaces, a radical idea at the time, and one which required an unusual agility of mind and response to human requirements. The exterior of Hill House, with its appearance of a Scottish farmhouse, does not, however, prepare the visitor for its innovative interior.

A small entrance space leads by three steps along a trellised wall to the main hall, a long rectangular space with a high ceiling with dark beams, from which are suspended large square light fixtures shaped like box kites. The effect is startling and original and the rectilinear lights are echoed in the carpet design. On one side of the hall is a dark side table with legs reminiscent of Japanese furniture.

One of the dark doors in the light-coloured wall leads to the library, an important room for a publisher, which also served as his study. There is a decidedly masculine feel about the room with its dark shelves filled with books whose spines give a muted touch of colour to the walls, and more colour is subtly suggested by small glass panels set into the doors.

The bedrooms of the house reflect, by contrast, the feminine side, full of light colours and curved surfaces. The space of the main bedroom is divided into a recess for the bed under a low ceiling and was perhaps meant to be separated from the rest of the room by a curtain. The room is illuminated by two windows between which is a tall, dark ladder-back chair. The fireplace, essential in the days before central heating, is by the entrance door which has an elegant white surround, with a recess rather like an inglenook.

Recalling the building of the house, Walter Blackie wrote some years later that, as he took possession of the completed property and settled up with Mackintosh, he had been surprised to find that the whole project had come in under the budget agreed. This was not remarkable to those who knew that Mackintosh was a man of rare integrity whose honesty was only equalled by his stubbornness in refusing to compromise his aesthetic ideals.

His work on Kate Cranston's Willow Tea Room in

OPPOSITE and ABOVE
Windyhill (1900)

Though much smaller than
The Hill House, Windyhill is
imbued with Mackintosh's
strong feeling for the soft
Scottish vernacular
architecture and at first
glance the exterior is not
unlike a farmhouse. The
interior, however, bears the
stamp of Mackintosh's
very own idiosyncratic
style.

Windyhill

RIGHT
The charming drop light
with its oriental-looking
shade is a perfect foil for
the latticed window in the
entrance porch. Each of
the leaded squares in the
window is slightly different
and the three rectangular
pieces of glass at the top
break up the design in an
interesting way.

BELOW
The hallway looking
towards the stairs.

RIGHT and BELOW
An area of seating on an
upstairs landing.

The Hill House, Helensburgh (1904)

Unlike many of his contemporaries, such as Anderson and Lorimer in Scotland and Lutyens in England, Mackintosh never achieved a large practice for domestic architecture; but The Hill House, which he built for the publisher Walter Blackie, demonstrated his capabilities superbly. The simplicity and style of the exterior was rivalled only by its dazzling interior.

Sauchiehall Street and on The Hill House had left Mackintosh exhausted and with eye strain and he and Margaret took a holiday in the Orkneys. On their return he was asked by Kate Cranston and her husband, Major Cochrane, to redecorate their house, Hous'hill at Nitshill, to his own design (p. 104–105).

Since the house was already standing there was no question of redesigning the building, but Mackintosh created new interior decoration and furniture. In the large living room he divided the space in two with a see-through lattice-work screen. To illuminate both areas he designed a cylindrical light with a rectilinear frame and in order to create more room in one of the two new spaces, he designed a set of chairs in dark wood with high vertical backs.

In a bedroom he departed from the light atmosphere and introduced a four-poster bed with blue uprights and a large blue settee at its foot. The chairs, with blue lattice-work backs, complemented the rest of the decor, but the writing desk and occasional table were in polished wood. Another bedroom was in pale colours with two four-poster beds and there were also lattice-backed chairs and some elegant candlesticks. Unfortunately, like so much of Mackintosh's work, the Nitshill designs were lost in a fire, but were recreated from photographs.

A final opportunity to combine Mackintosh's architectural and interior design skill arose in an ill-fated project, when he was asked to construct a house for the Shand family. There seems to have been an early misunderstanding, for the Shands were looking for a design in the Tudor style, which was then fashionable but which Mackintosh abhorred. Though Mackintosh began the design, the upshot of the disagreement between architect and client

The Hill House

OPPOSITE
OPPOSITE
The entrance hall to the house is a Mackintosh tour de force which gives the visitor the impression they are entering a baronial residence, but which is both friendly and welcoming. The ceiling beams in dark wood are a little sombre but are illuminated by the light fittings which float in the air like box kites.

LEFT
There is a distinct polarization between the masculine and feminine elements in The Hill House, and this room is undoubtedly masculine, and almost resembles a boardroom. However, the buffet laden with china tells us that it is in fact the dining room.

was that Mackintosh was replaced by another architect.

The affair virtually brought Mackintosh's domestic architecture to a halt and he now found it difficult to find work. No doubt this was largely due to the fact that he was at odds with the popular architecture of the time and that his potential clients were not attuned to the modern movements in art and design that were taking place in Europe. There was also his character, his Scottish Presbyterian integrity, which was difficult to compromise when he thought he was right. Sadly, he had begun to drink heavily; whether it was as a result of disappointment over the dashing of his early hopes of changing the face of Scottish architecture, the Byronic effect of a malformed foot, or some genetic weakness, such as autism, is not clear; but it evidently made relationships with his wife and clients difficult.

It was some years, therefore, before he had another chance to design a house and in the meantime, following a disagreeable experience at Walberswick, he moved to London.

The Hill House

The vaulted recess in the main bedroom, initially to be enclosed by leaded-glass screens and gossamer curtains designed by Margaret Macdonald Mackintosh, is a world of private sensuality; it has its own small window to the left, and the full-blown roses around the walls add a feminine quality to the white interior. ABOVE is a detail of one of two silk appliqué banners which hang either side of the bed.

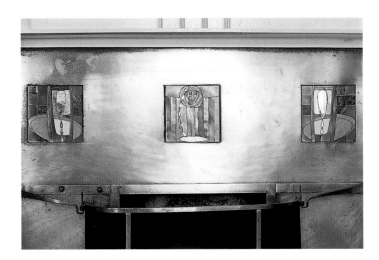

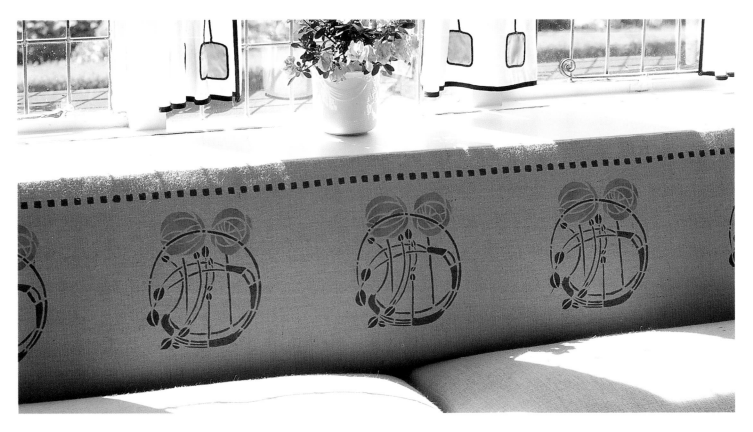

The Hill House

TOP LEFT
Detail of the fireplace in the master bedroom.

TOP RIGHT
The extravagant proportions of the high-backed chair is in dramatic contrast to the cool, pale room which has the required restful atmosphere and the touch of femininity which suggests Margaret Macdonald's collaboration.

ABOVE and OPPOSITE
The wide windows of the drawing room not only flood the room with light but also delight the eye with the delicacy of the curtains and the comfortable window seat ranged beneath.

The house that Mackintosh was commissioned to redesign in 1915 belonged to Whynne Bassett-Lowke (p. 106–107), an engineer who manufactured accurate models of trains which were coveted by both young and old enthusiasts alike. The house was at 78 Derngate in Northampton and owing to the restrictions of wartime, could not be rebuilt, so Mackintosh's contribution was limited to interior decoration. As far as the exterior was concerned, Mackintosh opened up larger window spaces at the rear to increase the interior illumination, but this was all.

He increased the space in the hall by replacing the wall separating the stairs from the hall by a lattice-work screen and introducing modern and unobtrusive lighting fixtures. The most startling feature of the new decor was in the guest room where Mackintosh introduced a design in black stripes which rose vertically from behind the recessed bed up to the ceiling, where it continued in a further transverse pattern of

more stripes. This motif was repeated in the bedclothes and the dark ladder-back chairs, which contrasts with the polished wood of the bedstead. The whole effect is aggressively masculine and quite different from the bedrooms he had previously designed with Margaret.

One of Bassett-Lowkes' guests, soon after the room was redesigned, was George Bernard Shaw, the writer and playwright, and perhaps the host was anxious to know if he had found the decor disturbing: the famous celebrity replied that he had not, for he always slept with his eyes shut.

The Hill House

OPPOSITE
The ground-floor library leads off the entrance hall and, like the hall, has a masculine appearance with oak bookshelves and panelling. The panels are discreetly decorated with squares of purple glass, offset by a stylized bending reed form, and add a touch of lightness to the serried ranks of books.

RIGHT and BELOW
The magnificent writing desk designed by Charles Rennie Mackintosh for Hill House, shown closed and open. Mackintosh was so pleased with the design that he had another made for himself.

Hous'hill, Nitshill (1904)

LEFT
Kate Cranston's house in which she lived with her husband, Major Cochrane, was redesigned by Mackintosh in 1904. Much of the furniture was already there but Mackintosh reorganized the spatial relationships of the house and added his own features, such as the lights hanging over the dining table.

RIGHT
The see-through screen in the drawing room, with its vertical slats, was Mackintosh's way of breaking up the space without reducing the amplitude of the whole. The cylindrical light illuminates both parts of the room which could consequently be used as two sitting areas

ABOVE
This desk was designed by
Mackintosh for the blue
bedroom at Hous'hill.

**78, Derngate,
Northampton, England**
(1915)

ABOVE
By now living in Chelsea,
Mackintosh was asked to
redesign W.J. Bassett-
Lowke's house. He
opened a wider window at
the rear of the building and
with the extra light that this
gave to the interior,
redecorated the hall with a
white fireplace and curtains
and wallpapers of his own
design.

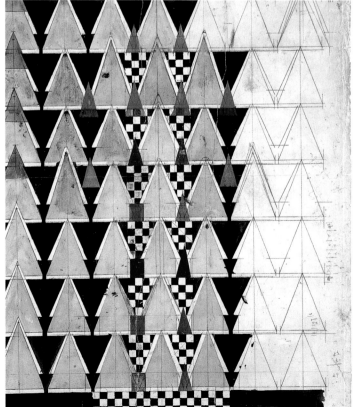

LEFT
Mackintosh's curtain and
wallpaper designs for the
hall at Derngate indicate
that he was leaving the Art
Nouveau style behind and
evolving one in which
nature and the industrial
world were beginning to
merge. However, he
softened the machine-like
regularity of the pattern by
introducing subtle
variations.

The guest bedroom in the home of Whynne Bassett-Lowke, the engineer and model railway maker, was one of Mackintosh's more fantastic and daring creations. The dark parallel lines seem to echo the railways for which Bassett-Lowke was famous and the gleaming wood of the bedsteads evoke the splendours of first-class travel.

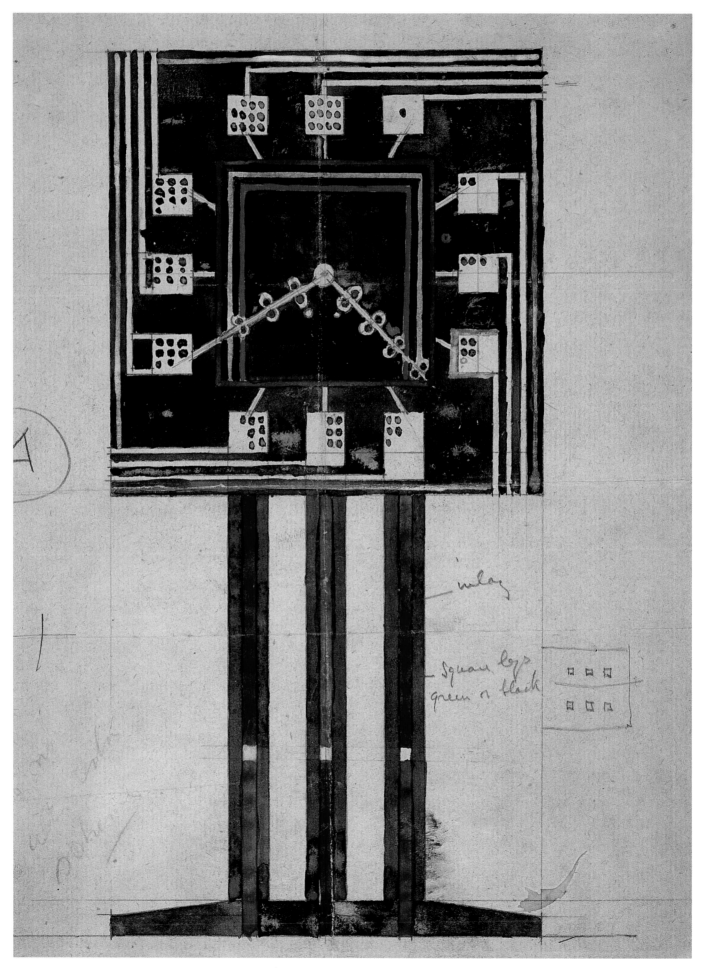

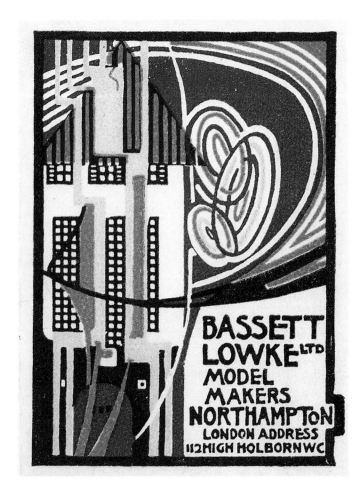

OPPOSITE

Design for a clock

(c.1917–23)

Watercolour and pencil on laid paper.

The clock was intended for W. Bassett-Lowke, the owner of 78, Derngate, Northampton, which Mackintosh had renovated earlier.

ABOVE and RIGHT

Designs for an advertising label (c.1919)

Red, blue and black ink on adhesive paper.

Apart from these, Mackintosh produced other designs for W. Basset-Lowke, including a cigarette box and Christmas cards.

CHAPTER SEVEN
BACK TO NATURE

RIGHT

Apple, Walberswick

(1915)

Watercolour and pencil on paper.

Although Mackintosh drew flowers all his life, the drawings he produced in Walberswick, from 1914–1915, were to absorb him completely and become the centre of his existence. This drawing, precisely observed in a botanical sense, would not look out of place on a delicate Chinese teapot.

OPPOSITE

Spurge, Withyham (1909)

Watercolour on paper.

This was made during a visit to East Sussex and is a complex composition of overlapping forms, delineated by colour washes. The spurge, or euphorbia, with its acid-green bracts, is centrally placed, with vinca and rhododendron flowers to the sides.

After the early years, which had been so full of promise, when Mackintosh had received so much admiration from his friends of the Secession in Vienna, Munich and Dresden, and had been commissioned by Scottish enthusiasts like Francis Newbery, William Davidson, Walter Blackie and Kate Cranston, his lack of success during the first decade of the 20th century was a bitter disappointment. This must have been deepened by the knowledge that in France Guimard was redesigning the Paris Métro and a number of buildings, including new department stores, while in the Netherlands Victor Horta's Art Nouveau style was much in demand and Tiffany in New York was setting a new fashion in domestic furnishings.

Bouts of depression made such work that came his way difficult to conclude and as a result his relationship with Honeyman and Keppie came to an end. Concerned by what the future might hold, he transferred ownership of the house in Florentine Terrace to Margaret, and decided to leave Glasgow in an attempt to rebuild his self-confidence.

On the eve of the Great War in 1914, he and Margaret went to Walberswick, a small village near Southwold in Suffolk. This was a small artist's colony and the Newberys had a property there in which the Mackintoshes took up residence for the summer. Here, in a landscape of heath and sea and with the vast expanse of sky which had fascinated Constable, the Mackintoshes lived frugally on a small amount of money that Margaret had inherited and they painted the wild flowers together along the low cliffs.

Since it was a time before the use of herbicides was widespread, the fields were full to overflowing with native flora and fauna. Both the Mackintoshes worked assiduously, recording the various kinds of flowers and grasses in paintings which were in a naturalistic style. It was as if, having had his creative design ideas rejected, he and Margaret had decided to return to the very source of nature for their inspiration.

Among the native plants were fritillarias, whose spring buds burst out in slender tendrils of leaves and violet flowers, the thorny berberis, the cuckooflower, or lady's smock, and

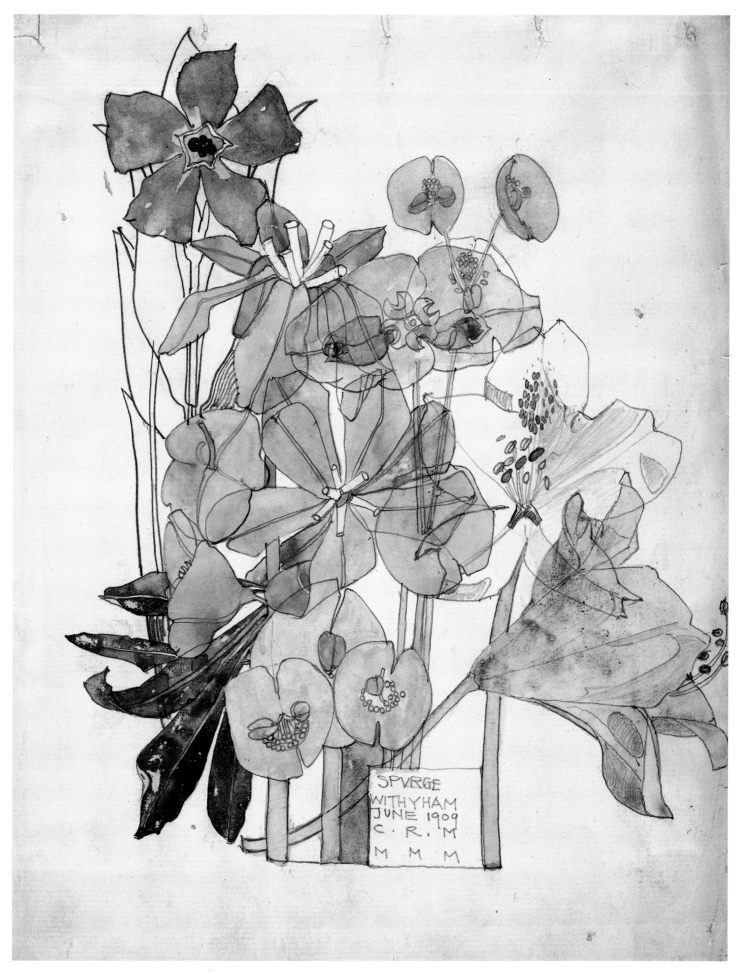

SPVRGE
WITHYHAM
JUNE 1909
C . R . M
M M M

ABOVE

Blue and Pink Tobacco Flowers on a Green Lattice (c.1915–28)
Pencil and watercolour on brown tracing paper.

Mackintosh never ceased to be fascinated by shapes and colours and was endlessly inventive with them. In fact, most of his best ideas came from nature. At Walberswick, with plenty of time on his hands, he whiled away the hours studying wild flowers and shrubs, which came in useful when he later began to design textiles.

the thrift or sea pinks which inhabited the shore. Nearly all their drawings bear the initial CRM and MMM, poignant proof of their close relationship at this difficult time.

Mary Newbery, daughter of Francis, who had known Mackintosh when she was a young girl and her father was director of the Glasgow School of Art, had visited Vienna and knew something of the admiration felt there for Mackintosh. Meeting him now at Walberswick, where she was staying the summer at her parents' house, she was sad to find that Mackintosh appeared to have lost heart, though she did not remark on the fact. She spoke out after his death, lamenting the waste of talent and Scotland's loss of the great buildings Mackintosh would now never create.

The Mackintoshes, however, never completely lost faith, and their devotion to their native culture never wavered. In all his work Mackintosh had resisted the temptation to follow foreign leads and become a fully committed Symbolist or a devotee of Art Nouvea. It had been his ambition to create a new art out of the tradition of his native land.

While Mackintosh was wandering in the wilderness,

OPPOSITE

Japonica (1910)
Watercolour.

This study of Japanese quince, made at Chiddingstone, Kent, has oriental overtones similar to the apple blossom on page 110. Overall, colour is used sparingly to give particular importance to the orange-scarlet flowers.

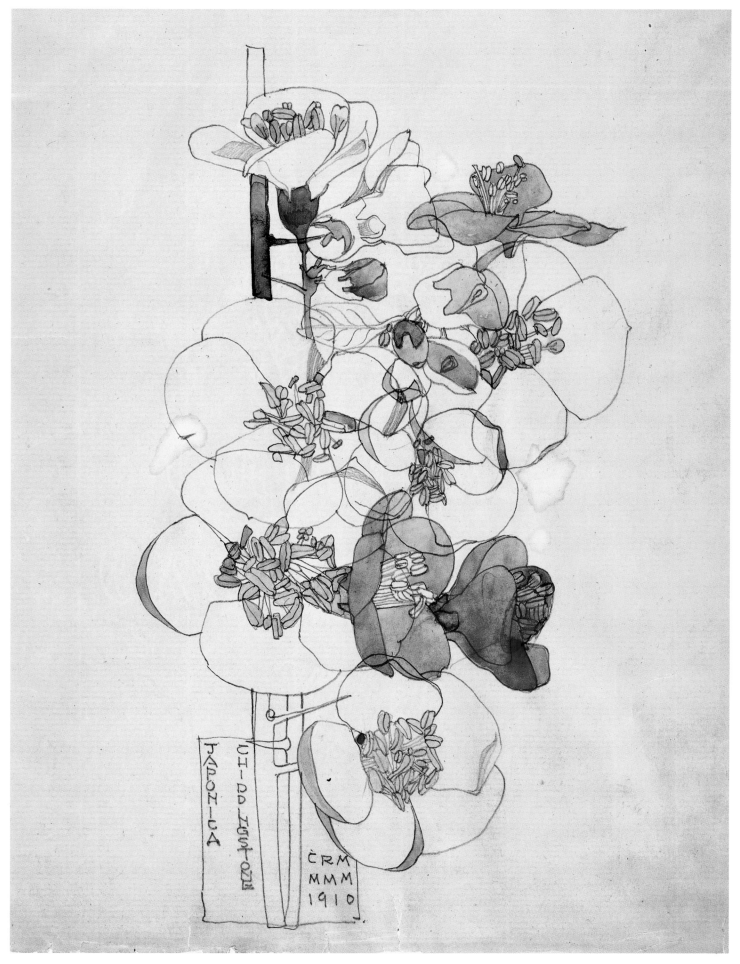

ABOVE

Venetian Palace,

Blackshore-on-the Blyth

(1914)

Watercolour on paper.

One of the few paintings
from Mackintosh's period
at Walberswick which was
not a flower study, its title
is a wry parody of a
Venetian canal scene. This
was the last known work
to be exhibited in Scotland
before Mackintosh moved
to England and was shown
at the Royal Academy in
London in 1923.

great changes had been taking place abroad but were being
virtually ignored in Britain until in 1910 a young art critic
and painter called Roger Fry suggested to the director of the
Grafton Gallery in London that he should put on a show of
French art. The show consisted of paintings by Cézanne,
Matisse, Derain, Gauguin, Seurat and the young Picasso,
none of whom were particularly famous at the time, and
proved a sensation, though it was described by some critics as
disagreeable pornography and by others as a collection of
meaningless daubs.

This was followed by an exhibition of the work of Paul
Gauguin at the Stafford Gallery, which was recorded by the
painter Spencer Gore and confirms that among those present
were Augustus John, Walter Sickert, Philip Wilson Steer and
other Chelsea bohemians, all of whom represented the avant-
garde of the new British art movements.

Mackintosh, in his depressed isolation in Glasgow and
then at Walberswick, seems to have been unaware of the art

OPPOSITE

Gilardia (1914)

Watercolour on paper.

Another Walberswick
painting, this may actually
be a gaillardia, as
Mackintosh occasionally
made mistakes when
naming plants.

GILARDIA
WALBERSWICK
1 9 1 4
C R M

OPPOSITE

Design for a printed textile (c.1915–1923)
Watercolour.

Both Mackintosh and his wife, Margaret Macdonald, habitually used the rose motif in their designs, examples being the Rose Boudoir (p. 36 and 37) and Windyhill (p. 89). It appears to have been a symbol of their love and artistic collaboration, so it was natural for Mackintosh to extend its use to textiles.

LEFT

Daisy (1915)
Watercolour on paper.

It is hard to believe that a painting of such supreme delicacy could have been produced outside China or Japan. This is another of Mackintosh's Walberswick pictures and he placed his wife's initials on them to indicate that she was present when he painted them.

revolution taking place in France and transported to London by Fry. There is no evidence in his work of the dramatic Picasso and Braque experiments with Cubism or the unleashing of colour by Matisse and his friends, whose explosive use of unmixed primary hues caused them to be named Les Fauves – the wild beasts.

It seemed as though Mackintosh's artistic world had been reduced to the narrow environment of Walberswick where he had found peace and an opportunity to recover his shattered dreams. It was a shock, therefore, on returning one day from a day's drawing on the beach, when he found a soldier with fixed bayonet at his door and police rifling through his cottage and studio where they had discovered letters from his friends in Germany and Austria, and which were confiscated for closer examination. It appeared that in a frenzy of wartime hatred of the enemy, suspicion had grown of anyone not a bona fide member of the small community, and the rumour was that Mackintosh was a spy.

The reasons for these suspicions were many: the Mackintoshes were artists, a fact which in itself was thought

RIGHT
Campanula (1914)
Watercolour and pencil on paper.

OPPOSITE
Willowherb (1919)
Watercolour and pencil on paper.

peculiar among farm workers and fishermen; they spoke with an odd accent (Glaswegian was as foreign as German to the locals); and Mackintosh himself looked rather odd, dressed in a large black cloak, as he made his limping way along the beach. There was no doubt in the villagers' minds that Mackintosh was sending information abroad or even signalling to submarines, such was the hysteria in 1915 born of fear of invasion. The upshot of the affair was that Mackintosh and other artists living and working along that stretch of coast were asked to move away, forcing them to take refuge in London.

WILLOW
HERB

BUXSTEAD
1 9 1 9
CRMMMM

CHAPTER EIGHT

LONDON & ABROAD

L ondon, where the Mackintoshes were welcomed and encouraged by their friend, Patrick Geddes, was a city where strict Victorian principles had to a large extent softened during the short reign of Edward VII, whose popularity and dedication to pleasure had encouraged a more liberal approach to life.

Social life in London now included the theatre with George Bernard Shaw's daring comedies and satires, in which matters not usually raised in polite society were openly discussed. Then there were the innovative ballets of the Russian, Diaghilev, with avant-garde music by Igor Stravinsky, while the world of literature saw the novels of a young working-class writer called D.H. Lawrence, whose frank exploration of sexual relationships and condemnation of the ills of industrial society, as in *Sons and Lovers* (1913), gave rise to a whole new climate of debate. In other words, a new era had begun.

There are no records of the Mackintoshes' opinion of the status quo when they gravitated to London in 1915, but since they were Scottish and Presbyterian one can only suspect that they either did not approve or preferred not to be involved.

The Mackintoshes rented a studio in Glebe Place, Chelsea and, as they could not sleep there, took a room in Oakley Street near a café called the Blue Cockatoo, where they took meals in the congenial company of other artists, which included Augustus John and his set. Though they did not fit easily into the London scene, they began to feel at ease and were encouraged by being able to work and earn money again.

They were still living frugally on Margaret's small allowance, but the flower drawings made at Walberswick now began to provide material for designs which they were able to sell to textile manufacturers, supplying the needs of a post-war generation who wished to furnish their homes in the new style which had grown from the efforts of the Secessionists

OPPOSITE

The Village, Worth Matravers (1920)

Watercolour on paper.

ABOVE

The Downs, Worth Matravers (1920)

Watercolour on paper.

When the Mackintoshes lived in London they would sometimes visit

Mackintosh's old friend and mentor, Francis Newbery, who now lived in the village of Corfe Castle in Dorset. These two landscapes were produced on such a visit, Mackintosh appearing to have made the full transition from architect to painter.

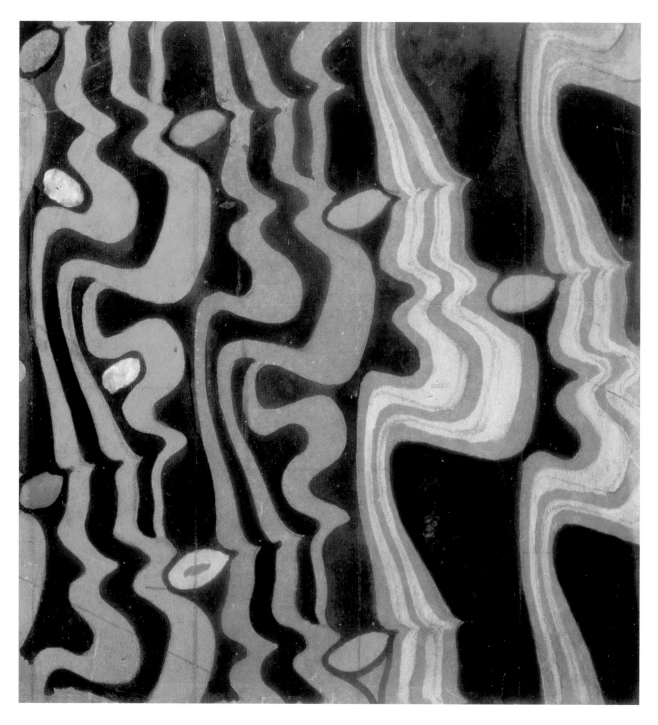

ABOVE

Textile Design

(c.1915–23)

Watercolour and pencil on paper.

Although Mackintosh's departure from Walberswick had been unexpected and unpleasant, the sojourn by the sea had helped heal his bruised spirits and when he arrived in London he began to work on textiles, some of which were offered to Liberty of London and other commercial outlets. This enabled the Mackintoshes to live modestly within the

OPPOSITE

Stylized Tulips

(c.1915–23)

Watercolour and pencil on brown tracing paper.

The tulip shapes in this proposal for a textile design are barely discernible among the flowing abstract forms, to which Mackintosh has added a lively interest with variations of colour and technique.

Still Life of Anemones
(c.1916)
Pencil and watercolour.
19⁷/₈ x 19¹/₂in (50.5 x
49.5).

Both Mackintosh and
Margaret were interested
in textiles around this time
and other artists they met
in London were

encouraging them to try
out new ideas. However,
Mackintosh had still not
abandoned his flower
paintings, though one of

his new and lively textile
designs is shown reflected
in a mirror in the
background.

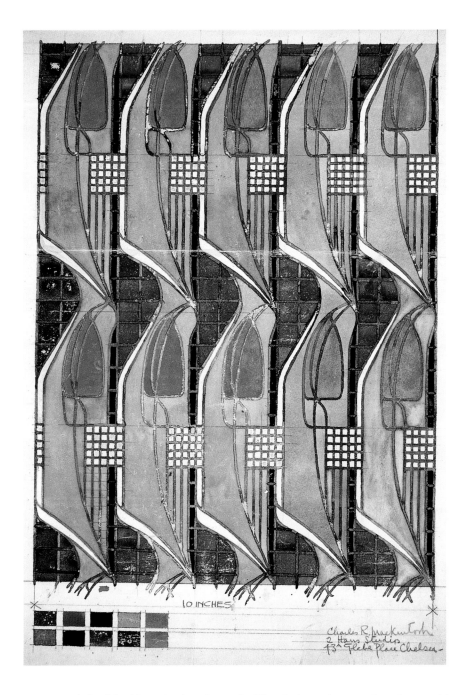

Tulip and Lattice

(c.1915–23)

Watercolour and pencil on paper.

Many of Mackintosh's textile designs were not printed in his lifetime but and the Mackintoshes' early work. The designs they produced were not realistic but brought into play their individual talent for design, which had earned them an international reputation.

In more confident mood, Mackintosh had also begun to enter his work in exhibitions: at the International Society of Sculptors, Painters, and Gravers, at the Arts and Crafts shows, and in America in Detroit and Chicago. Establishing himself in London had not been easy but he received a commission in 1920 to design a studio for the artist Harold Squire at Glebe Place, and for the Arts League of Service, a building which would have been a fine addition to the Chelsea scene but which was never realized because, according to Mary this one became available in 1990 when Mackintosh's rare talent was becoming recognized, and much of his work on houses and interiors was being collected or reconstructed.

Newbery, the London County Council thought it too plain.

In view of the difficulties Mackintosh was experiencing in pursuing his architectural career, he decided to turn to painting for which there was a new market. The art-buying public, influenced by the cultural breakthrough of Roger Fry, were eager to establish a new post-war lifestyle of their own and had begun to buy *plein-air* landscapes in a style derived from the Impressionists. Among the new works soon to be seen in dealers' windows were those by Walter Sickert, Spencer Gore and Harold Gilman, known at the Camden Town group, and there were others like the Nash brothers, Paul and John, and the young Stanley Spencer and his brother Gilbert.

Though still making designs for textiles, and book jackets for Walter Blackie, Mackintosh began to spend more time painting landscapes in the southern counties of Britain, those surviving being views of Worth Matravers in

OPPOSITE
White Roses (1920)
Watercolour on paper.

At first sight this could be taken for a traditional flower painting, complete with dainty porcelain bowl, until one notices bold elements of Mackintosh's developing textile designs creeping into the background.

ABOVE
Bouquet (c.1918–20)
Watercolour and pencil on paper.

These highly stylized, almost jazzy flowers were possibly intended as a design to be printed on silk or chiffon for dress fabrics, or on heavier materials suitable for curtains or upholstery.

Collioure (1925)

Watercolour on paper.

By the 1920s, Mackintosh was becoming increasingly disenchanted with London, where he seemed to be making little progress and was feeling at odds with the world, especially where architecture was concerned. It is thought that the Mackintoshes were in France from about 1923–1927, where they based themselves in the Pyrénées-Orientales. Collioure is a picturesque fishing village not far from Port-Vendres, where Mackintosh produced most of his work in France. Ironically, although this self-isolation allowed him to paint, it did nothing to promote his public image.

Dorset. He was embarking on a new career which would occupy him for the rest of his life.

A photograph of Mackintosh at this time shows a well-built, middle-aged man with white hair, formally and carefully dressed and wearing a high collar and cravat. He could be mistaken for a senior civil servant or industrial magnate were it not for the fact that he is also wearing a dark cape, which gives him a distinctly bohemian air. He does not look like a man who has been the victim of ill-fortune; in fact, life had improved for him lately and he had the challenge of a new venture ahead.

At the suggestion of J.D. Fergusson, a fellow Scot and painter, who belonged to a group interested in the Matisse experiments with colour, the Mackintoshes decided to travel in the south-west of France where it would be possible to enjoy a better life on their meagre income. They went to Amélie-les-Bains, a small town in the Pyrenees, to Ille-sur-Têt, near Mont Louis, where Mackintosh painted the mountain valleys, working slowly but with intense concentration. The area of the Pyrenees were almost unknown to the British at the time and the Mackintoshes seemed lost to their friends who found it hard to imagine where and why they were there. In the winter they visited the Mediterranean coast and stayed at small ports of the Rousillon, an area that had once been part of the domain of the Counts of Barcelona. In these tranquil places, apart from the high months of summer, they settled at Port-Vendres, near Collioure, where Matisse, Signac and Derain had experimented with colour between 1905 and 1907.

Mackintosh, now nearing 60, was disinclined to indulge in youthful experiments; he and Margaret settled into the Hôtel du Commerce at Port-Vendres and he began work in the way he knew best, as a draughtsman with an architect's eye for structure. Unlike Cézanne, whose interest in structure was resolved by the manipulation of colour, in terms of hues and tones, Mackintosh created his compositions by means of meticulous draughtsmanship.

Mackintosh produced 46 paintings during these last years of his life, half of them of Port-Vendres where, by 1927, he was on his own, as Margaret was in London for medical treatment for a heart complaint. Her absence affected him deeply.

Since the days of The Four, Margaret had been Mackintosh's lover, his intimate companion and work partner, and he had begun to depend on her more and more. It would appear, from the fact that they lived in separate rooms at the hotel, that she had resigned herself to a less than perfect life and that she had given up painting. She had remained loyal and supportive but had lost opportunities and her husband's heavy drinking must have worried her deeply.

RIGHT
The Rock (1927)
Watercolour and pencil on paper. 12 x 14½in (30.5 x 36.8cm).

This painting, one of the last painted by Mackintosh at Port-Vendres, shows a mound of layered rocks with the town in the background separated by a stretch of water that gives an unusual point of view to the scene. Mackintosh appears to have painted the town of Port-Vendres first, superimposing the rocky outcrop in a highly dramatic and striking way.

LEFT
Le Fort Maillert, Port-Vendres (1927)
Watercolour on paper.

Mackintosh approaches the grim fort atop its rocky eyrie no longer as an architect but as a painter, giving the striated rock an almost abstract form, and a strength and grandeur that augured well for the future. Margaret, who had been in London for medical treatment, had made contact with the Leicester Gallery hoping to organize a show of her husband's work; but his death in 1928 brought an end to this happy prospect.

The Little Bay, Port-Vendres (1927)
Watercolour and pencil on paper.

This intimate view is one of Mackintosh's most delightful paintings of Port-Vendres. It combines the reality of the scene with the discipline of an abstract composition that is the framework that makes it a good painting. The diagonal rail in the foreground, the curve of the little waves along the shore, and the firm rectilinear buildings all combine to stimulate and satisfy the eye of the viewer.

132

Collioure (c.1927)
Watercolour and pencil on paper.

Mackintosh appears to have travelled light when out painting, unencumbered by easels, stools or umbrellas. He took with him the bare necessities of water bottle, watercolours, palette and brush, his method of working being to sketch in the outlines of the composition using pencil. Watercolour would then be applied and the pencil marks erased.

Both appeared to have accepted their lot: when a visitor arrived at Port-Vendres and asked Mackintosh how things were going, he replied that he was as happy as a sandboy. Whatever their personal situation, they kept it to themselves.

Mackintosh had never been a man to communicate his personal thoughts easily; some students of his life think that this was on account of his autism, though he was also known to be naturally introverted and reclusive.

Meanwhile, Mackintosh was spending hours in the open air, studying the scene before him. He had already painted several views from the window of the hotel, looking across at the quays and tall terraces of houses of the harbour; his

ABOVE

Steamer Moored at the Quayside, with Two Gendarmes Standing

(c.1927)

Watercolour and crayon on paper.

The two gendarmes are probably the only two figures that Mackintosh ever included in his paintings, which are usually devoid of people and animals. The style of the painting, with its heavy defining lines, was popular in Paris and had been used by such painters as Marquet and Dufy, both of whom had lived nearby at Collioure in the Fauve years.

OPPOSITE

A Southern Town

(1923–27)

Watercolour and pencil on paper.

In this painting Mackintosh has accentuated the light and shade effect in much the same way as the early Cubist painters. Painted in flat colour, the Cubist technique is marked, but Mackintosh's eye for detail, as in the windows and balconies, keeps the painting on a realistic level.

painting now had the flavour of Impressionism but with tighter handling and more muted colours. The atmosphere is static, there are no signs of people, not even a dog, which may have reflected something of his present state of mind.

Some time later he again used the façade of the houses across the harbour as a background to a freighter moored on the quayside. This time he used black lines to define his drawing in the style of the Parisian post-Impressionist painters from the Académie de la Palette. He only painted four harbour scenes and then settled on subjects that suited him better, including the rough landscape of Mont Louis in the Pyrenees or the rocky shore and the rooftops of local villages which had an architectural quality which suited him well.

Though the Mackintoshes had lost touch with almost all their friends in England, a tenuous link had been maintained with Francis Newbery, his wife Jessica and daughter Mary, now Mary Sturrock. Mary had always admired Toshie, as the family had called him since the days of the Glasgow School of Art, and she was deeply upset that he was experiencing difficulties in his career, caused, she thought, by the ignorance and hostility of people unsympathetic to the creative process. On his own, without Margaret, she worried that Mackintosh had become something of a lost soul.

Alone, Mackintosh was bereft and his desperate loneliness broke the reserve behind which he had damned up his life's disappointments and his strong unspoken feelings concerning

Margaret. He now wrote to her frequently, referring to his letters as 'The Chronicle', in which he recorded his daily life, the progress of his work, and his intense feelings of isolation.

His only friends at Port-Vendres were the Ihlees, a painter and his wife, and Monsieur Pous, the patron of the Hôtel des Templiers where Mackintosh would sit in the bar after his day's work. It was here too that he met Ihlee who told Mackintosh that he enjoyed his company because he was always so cheerful. True to his nature, Mackintosh was not going to complain to a stranger; but to Margaret he opened his heart. After the prosaic accounts of how a painting was going and what he had eaten for dinner, he signed off 'My Margaret, Your Toshie'. It was an echo of the days when the designs they created together were signed CRM/MMM.

He had now been working on one of his most interesting paintings, called *The Rock* (p. 131). This was a layered rock which stood across a strip of sea from Port-Vendres. He had been concentrating intensely on this work because, he wrote to Margaret, 'I intend to be a good painter.'

Then came a change of circumstances: he had been having trouble with a swollen tongue and had put this down to the quality of his pipe tobacco, blaming this on the Americans who had taken over the manufacture of the tobacco he had always smoked. 'Formerly it was light and fragrant and now it is sodden, sordid and sickening,' he wrote, and exploded with rage against Americans in general who worked only for millions (of dollars) and did not care for individuals. 'Damn them. Moving pictures. Architecture. Theatre.'

This uncharacteristic and unreasonable outburst was the symptom of a deeper malaise: a rage against life and destiny. A few days later he wrote to Margaret concerning some drawings she had left with *Homes and Gardens* magazine, who had delayed either accepting or rejecting them. Journalists, he told her, were blackguards. He expressed an even greater rage when confronted with an article concerning Reilly, 'a certain pompous bounder' who had crossed Mackintosh 30 years earlier, when he had worked for the assessors judging the Liverpool Cathedral entries and for whom Mackintosh had nurtured a lifelong hatred. 'I have waited patiently for 20 years to get one back on Reilly,' he wrote to Margaret, 'and during those 20 years I have never said a word against him to outsiders. Now I can get a few more nails in his nasty, stinking, cheap coffin.'

Port-Vendres, La Ville
(1924–26)
Watercolour on paper.

While in London, Mackintosh and Margaret received the sad news of the death of her sister Frances and it was thought that she had committed suicide. She and her husband, Bert McNair, had been working in Liverpool, but had found little success, and she had returned to Glasgow as a teacher, while McNair had begun to drink heavily. These misfortunes may have had some bearing on the Mackintoshes' decision to live abroad and settle in Port-Vendres in the Pyrénées-Orientales at the Hôtel du Commerce. Mackintosh painted this view of the town from their bedroom window. He always liked to paint with the subject in front of him, loath to rely on memory or sketches.

A few days later Mackintosh was filled with joy to hear that Margaret had recovered and was returning to Port-Vendres. He wrote her one last brief Chronicle: 'I don't think I have ever spent such a long, lonely time and I hope you will never need to go away for so long again.'

Margaret brought with her the good news that the Leicester Gallery in London were considering giving him an exhibition and life again seemed full of hope; but by the end of the summer his tongue was badly swollen and he returned to London to have his problem diagnosed as cancer.

After an operation, he and Margaret went to live in a house at Well Walk in Hampstead, but his remission was short-lived and he died the following year on 10 December 1928. He was cremated the following day at Golders Green Cemetery.

Margaret returned to Port-Vendres and took up painting again, but for a short time, for she died in 1933.

Slate Roofs (c.1925)
Pencil and watercolour.
14¹/₂ x 11in (37 x 28cm).

The houses in this painting are those of the village of Fetges, though it appears that Mackintosh has changed their position slightly in response to the demands of the composition. He has given greater prominence to the landscape, with its crystal-like rocks, than in the painting of Fetges, opposite, and the rocks in the foreground provide a unifying element to the whole.

Fetges (c.1926)
Pencil and watercolour.
18¹/₄ x 18in (46.4 x
45.7cm).

When he painted it,
Mackintosh considered this
to be his best work to date,
feeling that he had
mastered the technique of
painting the villages of the
Roussillon to which he gave
a universal aesthetic, while

retaining their local
character. Walter Blackie,
for whom Mackintosh had
designed The Hill House,
had remained a faithful
patron, and bought the
painting, presenting it to the
Tate Gallery, in London.

OPPOSITE
Pine Cones, Mont Louis
(1925)
Watercolour and pencil.

ABOVE
Mixed Flowers, Mont Louis (1925)

Watercolour and pencil on paper. 10^5/$_{16}$ x 8^1/$_{16}$in (26.2 x 20.5cm).

During his stay in France, Mackintosh continued to make studies of flowers and plants, these two from Mont Louis in the

Pyrenees being good examples. The bouquet of mixed flowers comprises many recognizable species, but Mackintosh has added a touch of humour to the composition by allowing birds' heads to emerge from closed buds.

141

P. 2–3, The Glasgow Picture Library: P. 4–5, Glasgow Picture Library: P 6, Scottish National Portrait Gallery, Edinburgh/The Bridgeman Art Library: P. 7, The Annan Gallery, Glasgow: P. 8, The Hunterian Art Gallery, University of Glasgow: P. 9, The Glasgow School of Art: P. 10–11, The Glasgow School of Art: P. 11 right, The Hunterian Art Gallery, University of Glasgow: P. 12–13 left, The Glasgow Picture Library, photographer Eric Thorburn: P. 13 right, The Hunterian Art Gallery, University of Glasgow: P. 14–15, The Glasgow Picture Library, photographer Eric Thorburn: P. 16, The Glasgow School of Art: P. 17, The Annan Gallery, Glasgow: P. 18, The Glasgow School of Art: P. 19, The Glasgow School of Art: P. 20, The Glasgow School of Art: P. 21, The Glasgow School of Art: P. 22, The Glasgow School of Art: P. 23, The Hunterian Art Gallery, University of Glasgow: P. 24 left, The Glasgow School of Art: P. 24 above, The Hunterian Art Gallery, University of Glasgow: P. 25, The Hunterian Art Gallery, University of Glasgow: P. 26, The Hunterian Art Gallery, University of Glasgow: P. 27, The Hunterian Art Gallery, University of Glasgow: P. 28–29, The Glasgow Picture Library: P. 30, The Glasgow Picture Library: P. 31 both, The Glasgow School of Art: P. 32–33, The Glasgow Picture Library: P. 34–35, The Glasgow Picture Library: P. 36, The Glasgow School of Art: P. 37, The Hunterian Art Gallery, University of Glasgow: P. 38, The Glasgow School of Art: P. 39, The Glasgow School of Art: P. 40–41, The Glasgow School of Art: P. 41 right, The Glasgow School of Art: P. 42, The Glasgow School of Art: P. 43, The Glasgow School of Art: P. 44, The Glasgow School of Art: P. 45 right, The Bridgeman Art Library: P. 46, The Glasgow School of Art: P. 47 above, The Bridgeman Art Library: P. 47 below, The Glasgow School of Art: P. 48, The Bridgeman Art Library: P. 49, The Glasgow School of Art: P. 50, The Bridgeman Art Library: P. 51 both, The Glasgow School of Art: P. 52–53, The Glasgow Picture Library: P. 54–55, The Hunterian Art Gallery, University of Glasgow: P. 56, The Glasgow Picture Library: P. 57, The Glasgow Picture Library: P. 58, The Glasgow Picture Library: P. 59 all, The Glasgow Picture Library: P. 60 left, The Glasgow Picture Library: P. 60–61, The Glasgow School of Art: P. 62–63, The Glasgow Picture Library: P. 64, The Glasgow Picture Library: P. 65, The Hunterian Art Gallery, University of Glasgow: P. 66–67, The Glasgow Picture Library: P. 68–69, The Glasgow Picture Library: P. 70, The Annan Gallery, Glasgow: P. 71, The Glasgow Picture Library: P. 72, The Glasgow Picture Library: P. 73 above, The Glasgow Picture Library: P. 73 below, The

Glasgow School of Art: P. 74, The Glasgow Picture Library: P. 75 above, The Glasgow Picture Library: P. 75 below, The Bridgeman Art Library: P. 76 above left and below, The Glasgow School of Art: P. 76 above right, The Bridgeman Art Library: P. 77 left, The Bridgeman Art Library: P. 77 right, The Glasgow School of Art: P. 78, top left, right and below, The Glasgow School of Art: P. 78–79, The Bridgeman Art Library: P. 80 all, The Bridgeman Art Library: P. 81, The Glasgow School of Art: P. 82, The Glasgow School of Art: P. 83, The Glasgow School of Art: P. 84–85, The Hunterian Art Gallery, University of Glasgow: P. 86–87, The Hunterian Art Gallery, University of Glasgow: P. 88–89, The Hunterian Art Gallery, University of Glasgow: P. 89 right, The Glasgow School of Art: P. 90, The Glasgow School of Art: P. 91, The Glasgow Picture Library: P. 92–93, The Glasgow Picture Library: P. 94–95, The Glasgow Picture Library: P. 96–97, The Glasgow Picture Library: P. 98–99, The Glasgow School of Art: P. 100–101, The Glasgow Picture Library: P. 102, The Glasgow Picture Library: P. 103 both, The Bridgeman Art Library: P. 104, The Hunterian Art Gallery, University of Glasgow: P. 105, The Bridgeman Art Library: P. 106 top Glasgow School of Art, P. 106–107, The Hunterian Art Gallery, University of Glasgow: P. 108–109, The Hunterian Art Gallery, University of Glasgow: P. 110, The Bridgeman Art Library: P. 111, The Hunterian Art Gallery, University of Glasgow: P. 112, The Hunterian Art Gallery, University of Glasgow: P. 113, The Hunterian Art Gallery, University of Glasgow: P. 114, The Hunterian Art Gallery, University of Glasgow: P. 115, The Glasgow School of Art: P. 116, Victoria & Albert Museum, London: P. 117, The Glasgow School of Art: P. 118, The Glasgow School of Art: P. 119, The Hunterian Art Gallery, University of Glasgow: P. 120–121, The Glasgow School of Art: P. 122, The Bridgeman Art Library: P. 123, The Hunterian Art Gallery, University of Glasgow: P. 124, The Bridgeman Art Library: P. 125, The Hunterian Art Gallery, University of Glasgow: P. 126–127, The Glasgow School of Art: P. 128–129, The Bridgeman Art Library: P. 130 left, The Glasgow School of Art: P. 130–131, The Bridgeman Art Library: P. 132, The Hunterian Art Gallery, University of Glasgow: P. 133, The Glasgow Picture Library: P. 134–135, The Hunterian Art Gallery, University of Glasgow: P. 137, Glasgow Art Gallery and Museum, Kelvingrove: P. 138, The Glasgow School of Art: P. 139, The Tate Gallery, London: P. 140, The Hunterian Art Gallery, University of Glasgow: P. 141, The British Museum, London.